C000264864

STABLE CONDITION

HOW TO STAY SANE WITH HORSE PEOPLE IN YOUR LIFE

DANIEL SKINNER

Illustrated by
LYNN ADAMS
Edited by
SIMON CLARK

OBVIOUS BOOKS

COPYRIGHT

Printed and bound in Great Britain by Clays Ltd, Elcograf S.p.A.

Published by Obvious Books, Bury St Edmunds

www.obviousbooks.co.uk

First Printing 2021.

ISBN 978-1-9164317-2-0

Illustrated by Lynn Adams

www.facebook.com/LynnAdamsIllustration

Read Skint Dressage Daddy online

www.skintdressagedaddy.com

www.facebook.com/skintdressagedaddy

THANKS

Firstly, I'd like to thank all of you who bought my last book and continue to follow and support me in all my silly nag-related projects. This spur-of-the-moment idea from four years ago was never supposed to be anything more than a quick joke, and the only reason it's continued to become a kind of second job is because of all of you who are so generous with your time and kind words.

I'd also like to thank Lynn Adams for once again providing the wonderful illustrations for this book. It really wouldn't be the same without them. And Simon Clark for, once again, helping me to cobble this thing together.

And of course, I have to thank the two women in my life — CC1 and CC2, without whom I'd have nothing to moan about but love dearly.

CONTENTS

CONTENTS

INTRODUCTION

For those of you that don't know me, I'm Skint Dressage Daddy. That's not my real name, by the way, that would be weird, it's just the stupid one I came up with in a moment of boredom a few years ago, sat in the cramped 'living' section of a cheap, rented horse trailer in a rain-soaked field while waiting for something to happen.

The 'something' in this case was the next round of a dressage competition that my daughter was entered into, so not even anything good. We were miles from home, parked in a wet and miserable field (did I mention that already?) and staring blankly into the mist and rain. Being made to watch horses walk up and down is bad enough, but this misery had been compounded by a spectacularly frustrating agenda that meant her two events for the day were scheduled for 8:30 am, the first of the day, and 4:30 pm, the last of the day. Clearly, the gods of dressage hated me. Or maybe just the organisers, but I've no idea what I could've done to upset them. Apart, perhaps, from turning up a day late without a valid ticket, getting turned away, sneaking in through the back, which spooked a horse that then ran off into some nearby woods before hiding my car between two others. But I think it was the gods.

And so, with the first damp prancing round over and done with, there was nothing to do but spend the next seven and a half hours cooped up out of the rain until 4:30. And when I say there was nothing to do, I really mean it. In situations like this, I find that after the seventh cup of tea and a doomed game of I-Spy ("Horse", "Horse", "Lorry", "Cloud", "Horse", *argument*), I tend to start moaning. Why were her two entries scheduled so far apart? Why wouldn't it stop raining? Why did I leave the comfort of my sofa to drive to this field? What's the fascination with sitting on a nag and walking in circles, anyway? How many cups of tea can you drink before you medically drown?

My other and better half, who I affectionately refer to as *CC1* (Cost Centre One) lowered her phone (a rare act) and glared at me.

'Stop moaning, for fuck's sake.'

I looked around the tiny space like a bored child who's been told to find something to do, lower lip thrust out and hands pushed deep into pockets as I surveyed the floor, ceiling and empty teacup.

'So what am I supposed to do then?' I asked, petulantly.

CC1 put her phone down with a deep sigh and fixed me with an impatient stare. It was clear that she was pretty much out of ideas herself though, and she started to join me in looking around with fingers tapping on the miniature table. Eventually, her gaze settled back on her phone, and it gave her an idea.

'I dunno... maybe set up a Facebook page and start

moaning on there instead. That should give me a break from having to listen to you.'

And so I did. By the magic of computer technology and mobile data tariffs, I set up a page with a hurriedly thought-of title and started moaning into my phone within about 30 seconds.

That was almost exactly four years ago as I write this, depressingly enough. The little girl, *CC2*, was 10 at the time, and a sweet little girl who was deeply obsessed with ponies and dressage. And so what became of her, I hear you ask? Did she leave that all behind, go off the rails and turn into a tearaway teenager, hanging around the bus shelter with the other proto-criminal dropouts, drinking cider and smoking stolen fags? Ha, no. I wish. No, sadly she stuck with the horses and became even more obsessed with all things nag-related, in turn bleeding my bank account dry and turning me into a rapidly greying borderline alcoholic who hasn't yet had the opportunity to stop moaning. I told you the gods of dressage hated me.

The Facebook page is still going and has led to several related projects, such as a column in a national horse magazine, an animated YouTube series and a range of other things that take up an inordinate amount of time without paying any actual money. Most relevantly though, was a book in 2018 which effectively summarised that first year of nag experiences into book form, and was much like the thing you're holding now, except less orange and more green.

You don't need to have read that one before reading this one or anything (although still available/all good bookshops etc), but this book continues on from where that left off and comprises my next three years of horse-based learnings. There's a general theme that flows through both books, which is the depressing expense of the whole damned nag business, and the constant attacks on my bank balance from all sides. I often think it would be easier for everyone if my forehead was fitted with a card slot and number keypad, and then the two CCs could just withdraw cash whenever they needed it, rather than needing to do all the plotting they currently do.

A lot of parents are very careful to avoid discussing financial matters in front of their children, to shield them from any potential worries that might weigh heavily on their young and innocent shoulders. CC2, on the other hand, is quite aware of what a financial burden she is, because I ensure I tell her regularly. There's no sugar-coating the situation, as far as I'm concerned, and I like to think I'm doing her a favour in preparing her for the shock of adult life when she has to start paying for some of this shit herself. I recall the first time I went to the dentist alone as a young adult, and the receptionist had to run after me as I walked out of the surgery because I wasn't aware that you have to pay once you're over 18. It was most awkward. I didn't even have the means to pay and had to leave my watch as security while I went to the nearest cash machine.

I'd hate for CC2 to have to experience similar embarrassed bill shock and be forced to leave some saddle or nag hat on a shop owner's counter and run screaming from the premises as it finally dawns on her that the money could instead pay for a year's rent or some exciting new drug habit. The only downside to keeping her so well-informed about the financial misery she forces on me and subsequently writing about it is that I fear she thinks the kind of purchases that reduce me to a sobbing, rocking mess are *good content*. A couple of years ago, sat at the dinner table, she asked me if I was going to write a second book.

'I don't know,' I said, chewing the idea over, 'I suppose it depends if there's anything to write about.'

'Mum!' she shouted with undisguised glee before standing up dramatically, 'We're going shopping!'

CHAPTER 1

Know your place

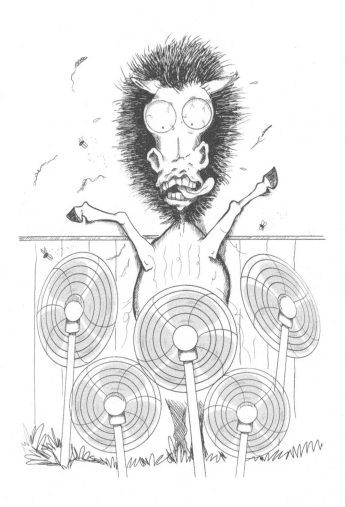

KNOW YOUR PLACE

It's very important to have goals in life, we're always being told this. When you're little, you're constantly asked what you want to be when you grow up, and at school, you have to make subject choices and get career advice. When you reach adulthood, you can't seem to move for posters featuring motivational slogans underneath photographs of whales, self-help books and endless Instagram photos of your annoying friends and their better holidays than yours.

When I was seven or eight, I dreamt of being a fighter pilot, but one of the nice ones that doesn't have to shoot at anybody and just gets paid to fly around all day, doing loops and stuff. In my teens, I decided I wanted to be a rock star and live a short but dramatic life of sex and drugs that would tragically end in a blaze of glory at 27, the result of a tremendous overdose of sex and/or drugs. At 26½ I changed my mind and decided that maybe something with good job security in a comfortable office might be better.

And so, life goes on, and your hopes and aspirations become steadily less dramatic. The heady dreams of fame, fortune and world domination you harboured in your youth become slowly replaced with aspirations of perhaps moving to a house with a utility room someday, and these goals continue their inevitable downwards trajectory until making it through a whole episode of Cash in the Attic without needing a wee makes for a pretty successful day.

For many people, though, the arrival of children can interrupt this trajectory and new parents often find that their goals in life have now changed. Sometimes these new goals are personal ones that are designed to make you a better parent. You know the kind, you read about them in irritatingly inspirational magazine interviews: get fitter/healthier/thinner so you can play football with your kids, or maybe give up smoking so you'll be around for longer, that kind of self-improvement rubbish. I have to confess, I did actually give up cigarettes when I became a parent, but only because I was planning to lecture them repeatedly about the dangers and cost of smoking from a young age and I didn't want to look like too much of a hypocrite so early on.

For other people, their new focus in life is essentially whatever their kids' goals are — good parents absorb the hopes and dreams of their children and do whatever they can in their power to facilitate them. Most people do this to a small degree just as part of basic parenting: they drive the kids to football practice every Saturday or save up to buy a piano, but the really dedicated ones reconfigure their whole lives in order to get little Jimmy onto a Formula One podium, or little Annabelle to the Olympics. This involves an enormous commitment of time, money and energy — using up all the life savings or taking on a second job and spending every waking hour driving up and down the country, or across the world.

Naturally, I dislike these kinds of perfect parents intensely, but I suspect that's because human nature tends to make us critical of people who are so clearly doing a better job than us. Or maybe that's just being English. I'm not sure, it might be a mixture. It's not that I'm a particularly *bad* parent, I don't think, but I am quite lazy. And quite tight.

So, you can imagine the creeping dread that's been a constant companion of mine for the last decade or so as CC2 has become, bit by bit, engulfed and consumed by a passion for horses and all things naguine. It's not like she even does anything interesting with them, like jump over stuff or go really fast on them. I could maybe get on board with that a little if there was some drama, perhaps a bit of danger. But no, her chosen sport is the formal prancing where people walk their nags from one part of a horse pitch to another, and her ultimate aim is to walk around slowly in a perfect circle. Yawn.

Of course, I want nothing more than to see her happy and her dreams fulfilled and all that bollocks. Really, I do. I mean, I plan to get old and incontinent at some point in the next 30 years, and I'll need her on side to look after me, so I think of this current stage as somewhat of an investment for the future, but I do often wish she could've chosen something a little more affordable to get addicted to. Gymnastics, perhaps, or the flute. Even skydiving, or quad bike racing, or heroin. Anything really where the hobby itself doesn't need its own house and food supply.

The thing is, I've come to terms with the fact that I'm middle-aged now, and my primary role in life is to provide for the children. It's probably a bit late to become a fighter pilot, or score a goal for England, or learn to play the drums. To be honest, I've been meaning to sort that box of

CDs into alphabetical order for nearly 20 years now, I should probably come to terms with the fact that it's never going to get done. I've moved house three times in that period too, I really should stop bringing it with me, especially as I haven't even owned a CD player for nearly a decade.

No, my job is to take a back seat in life and to provide for my family, and that's not so bad. I've come to accept my role as being someone in the background who doles out cash and drives people around, sort of like a philanthropic taxi driver, and this is standard for men at my stage in life, I suppose. It's the children that are important, not us.

What really pisses in my letterbox, though, is that I'm also on a rung well below the nag, and that's just taking things too far. It used to be a jokey complaint of mine around the house that the ponies are considered more important than me, but when it got to the point that everyone just shrugged and agreed, I had to stop saying it as all the impact had been lost.

Let me give you some kind of idea of what I'm talking about. The following is a conversation I had with CC1 recently:

Me: There's a letter there for you, by the way.
CC1: OK, thanks.

CC1 opens letter

CC1: Oh, it's just the dental report for the pony.
Me: The pony's got a dentist?
CC1: Er, yes.
Me: Amazing. So it regularly sees both a doctor

and a dentist, as well as a shoemaker. You'll be
telling me that it has a daily session with a
chiropractor next.

CC1: No, don't be ridiculous.

Me: Thank God for that.

CC1: It's just monthly.

Me: FFS. No wonder we never have any money.

CC1: Right, I've got to head out, I'll see you later.

Me: OK. Where are you going?

CC1: I have to get to the stables, the horse
masseur's due any minute. Oh, and if a lady turns
up while we're out, just tell her all the rugs are in
the garage — she'll be dropping off the clean ones.

Chiropractor, masseur, private dry-cleaning service.
The quality of life that nag has compared to me isn't even
a joke anymore. I thought horses were supposed to be
'beasts of burden', animals that humankind uses to make
life easier. Well, not in this house, it's completely the other
way round. I have to go out and work just so I can afford
to pay for its clothes to be cleaned and pressed. I've been
well and truly played by that horse, believe me, it must've
seen me coming.

I know what you're thinking — oh, here he goes again,
exaggerating wildly about the horses and the expense of it
all, blah blah blah, it can't be that bad. Well, we all went
out for a drive in the country the other day, the CCs, me
and the pony, and guess where we went? Fucking horse spa,
that's where.

Yes, that's right, the comfort of the nag hotel with the
private quarters and endless food supply wasn't enough for
the precious pony, and he had to be coaxed out into the
sunshine and gently chauffeured to some kind of luxury

nag retreat for the morning. The poor thing. Once there, he was lovingly washed, kitted out with some horsey swimming trunks and then led into a nag-sized jacuzzi where he spent some time relaxing in the bubbles while CC2 hand-fed him treats and stroked his face.

All I want to know is WHERE'S MY FUCKING JACUZZI??! Where's my spa retreat? Where are my massages? The last time I was fed treats while sat in a jacuzzi was... oh wait, that's right. NEVER! I've never been in a jacuzzi, I never get massages and the closest I've come to a sauna is when I open the dishwasher too early. I asked CC1 afterwards how much this spa session cost and she told me twenty quid, but she also did that shifty thing where she won't make eye contact and then suddenly remembers a text message she has to reply to urgently. This seems to happen quite a lot these days.

Now, you could argue that nags are finely tuned athletes that require a high level of care and maintenance to keep them fighting fit, whereas I just require wine and an adequate supply of Hobnobs, but I can't help feel that this is missing the point. Plus, I've watched dressage so there's no fooling me; even I could walk in a 20-metre circle without breaking a sweat, and I wouldn't need a massage and sauna afterwards. Though I wouldn't mind the offer from time to time.

It's not just in terms of high-end pampering that they outdo me, either, even his basic day-to-day comfort is considered significantly more important than my own. For example, as I write this, it is what we call 'summer', which for those of you reading from abroad is defined in the UK as more than two consecutive days without a yellow rain warning from the BBC. We missed out spring this year and just skipped straight from winter to summer in the space of a week, so I turned the heating off a fortnight ago and started padding around in shorts and flip-flops the next day, moaning about the flies and checking the freezer for any lollies left over from last year.

Unfortunately, our house isn't that good at moderating temperature. It's old, you see, and has none of those new-fangled inventions like insulation or effective heating, so is consequently freezing cold all winter and boiling hot all summer. There's sometimes a day around May time that's quite pleasant between about 2:30 and 3 pm, but otherwise, it's not really designed for human habitation. Usually, it's cold. And I mean c..o..l..d. It's hard to describe quite how cold it can get, but let's just say that we can't eat sandwiches in our house until April because that's when the butter defrosts.

I become a right Victorian Dad through the winter too. CC2 will regularly complain about being cold, and I'll admonish her sternly for not wearing enough clothes. According to her, it's a pain to use cutlery while wearing gloves and she's always moaning that her friends don't have to wear salopettes to bed. Kids today, eh?

If I was rich enough, I'd never be cold ever again. When I win the lottery, I'm going to move to the South of France for most of the year, but then I shall winter in the Caribbean, I think. You know you're rich when you get to use 'winter' as a verb.

But, for the foreseeable hour or two, it's summer, so tradition dictates that around this time of year I have to go into the *Cupboard of Doom* and get the fans out. The CoD is a big, cupboardy thing that's strangely roomy, and therefore jam-packed with a huge amount of useless old shit. It's like a walk-in version of that drawer in the kitchen with the dead batteries, the keys to forgotten locks, and the half-used pack of numbered birthday candles that you keep thinking will come in handy when someone reaches an age with a 4 or a 7 in it, but that you always forget when the time comes. The Cupboard of Doom is similar, but at a larger scale, and amongst the board games with the pieces missing and old scuba equipment (not joking btw) are the fans.

Like in most previous years, I prepared myself for the annual trip into the cupboard — torch, *check*; ball of string for finding my way out again, *check*; life insurance paid and up to date, *check*. I even made a packed lunch in case it took longer than usual to make my way past the off-cuts of carpet from when we did the landing and couldn't face throwing the leftovers away 'just in case'.

But this time was different. I worked my way through the forest of wrapping paper rolls with my machete in record time and even got past the fold-up camping chairs unscathed, but when I got to where the fans live, I was confused — there were no fans.

I traced my route back with the string and accosted CC1. 'Er... the fans have all gone. We've been burgled by some incredibly hot and specific thieves.'

CC1 stopped and thought for a minute.

'Oh yes, that's right,' she said. 'I remember now.'

'Go on,' I said slowly, my eyes narrowing.

'We took them to the stables last summer for the pony. He was hot.'

'Oh, he was hot, was he? He told you this, yes?'

She just shrugged and started to eat my packed lunch.

'But we had, like, four fans in there!'

'Yes, and the horse is quite big. He needed one for each corner.'

So this is basically where I am in life; I accrue a series

of dusty old fans over the years to ensure that I can perhaps be comfortable on a hot day, regardless of which room I'm in, but my lifetime of fan-collecting is nagated in a second because the poor, precious pony is more important than me and his comfort is paramount. I'm just grateful that the nag doesn't like watching TV, or listening to music or playing the guitar — all my worldly possessions would be gone in an instant and then nibbled to death. On second thoughts, maybe it's the other way round and I should be grateful that I don't enjoy licking salt blocks or eating hay, I'd probably never get to eat again.

On the subject of food, CC1 recently decided that we should look after ourselves a bit better and went all out to ensure we're eating as healthily as possible. To this end, she ordered a load of food online from some kind of specialist, organic health-food place. All the portions had to be carefully measured, weighed and matched to ensure each meal was nutritionally balanced and full of the very best, most expensive vitamins and minerals for healthy bodies and healthy minds.

Of course, I'm exaggerating when I say she decided 'we' should all eat healthily and expensively; she of course only meant the nag. I was left to continue living on beans and chips, as usual, no expense spent. As long as the pony is in tip-top condition, I can make do with scraps. It wouldn't surprise me if she started bringing some leftover hay into the kitchen and seeing if she could convince me that it's some kind of new, very thin pasta.

This new health kick for the horse doesn't just mean buying the new, super-expensive stuff and chucking it into his hotel room, either. Oh, no. Muttering something about 'nutrients', 'sugar content' and 'precious, precious, beloved pony', the hay has to be carefully soaked at exactly 16.2°c in a special mixture of 7 parts water, 2 parts asses' milk and 1 part mermaid tears, then gently steamed until it's *al dente* before each strand is checked by hand for imperfections and taste-tested for quality control. Once approved, the hay is hand-tied into bouquets and arranged *au haynet* before being personally delivered to the nag, who waits patiently at its hotel for the next meal.

I'm not joking about the steaming bit, either. Seriously, steamed! Like a serving of fucking artichokes at the Savoy! Apparently, the pony had a bit of a sore throat or something and it was absolutely vital that all his hay was steamed. Like he's the bastard Prince of Horses, or the one in the Lloyds advert. I asked CC1 how it gets steamed and she just pointed to a big, drum-shaped machine.

'Did we buy that?' I asked, suspiciously.

'No. Borrowed.'

But she did that thing again where she wouldn't meet my eye and then got her phone out.

In some ways, I wish I was a horse. I wish I was *our* horse, at any rate. I said before that I have to live on beans and chips, but to be honest, it's whatever I can find usually and/or cope with preparing. And we're usually out of chips. I had the stale bread crust, some dog biscuits and a single Quality Street I found down the back of the sofa for breakfast this morning.

I'm not expecting the CCs for dinner this evening as the nag's still awake and therefore needs stroking and mollycoddling. They're down at the hotel now, as usual. I've no idea what for, but probably to read him some poetry while doing his nails, or to run through this week's menu options. I, on the other hand, have been left at home to fend for myself. I don't know yet what I'm going to have for dinner but I've just remembered there's a bag of new birdseed in the shed I've been meaning to try out and I'm hopeful there are still more delights to find in the sofa, so it's not all doom and gloom. After that I might open the dishwasher early, I could do with some pampering.

Everything I've mentioned so far is really just day-to-day stuff for the nag, the kind of life it's become accustomed to. As my quality of life sinks ever downwards, his seems to be on an ever-upward trajectory, and this continues in the form of special occasions. CC2 has learnt to bake over the last couple of years and now loves to fill any spare evening or weekend afternoon with a session of baking delicious cookies. For the nag, of course.

I did manage to pinch one of these the other day and, although it initially tasted ok (if a bit too chewy and pepperminty for my liking), it went downhill pretty quickly and left a bitter taste that took hours to shift. Over dinner, CC2 casually mentioned that however tempted I might be, I was not to eat those cookies as they contained horse wormer. Who leaves poisoned cookies in a Tupperware container next to the bread bin?! With icing on! I mean, seriously, was it some kind of test? Is this some modern, equine version of a fairy tale and I now can't marry the princess or something? Either way, I suppose I've learnt my lesson — plus that insatiable hunger I've been having recently seems to have cleared up too, so that's something.

CC2 has a great deal of difficulty in understanding when she's spoiling the nag with all this unnecessary effort. Yesterday she got all stroppy because I made her do something that didn't involve horses. I can't remember what it was, something dull and unimportant, like doing homework or getting dressed.

'But I need to bake some treats, he's not had any today at all!' she whinged.

'He doesn't need to have treats every day,' I replied, 'that's what "treat" means. That's the whole point of them.'

'No, that's just human treats, my precious pony does!'

Honestly, this is how her brain works.

It goes without saying that he gets all kinds of presents for Christmas, and better ones than the socks I get, but special occasions don't end there. I got in trouble last year for not buying CC1 an Easter egg, so she took no chances this year and whisked CC2 away on a buying spree to get them all about three months in advance, including her own. Easter's a big deal for CC1; she's not religious, but she does believe in chocolate. I was considered too old for an egg (who's ever too old for a giant egg made of chocolate??) and instead got a bag of nuts as a consolation prize. I confess that I did enjoy them, but I wasn't the only one — they were open when I received them. It was kind of like 'Happy Easter, here's some nuts. They're really nice, by the way.'

After that, we all piled into the car to go for a drive to... guess where? Yep, the nag hotel. And can you guess what for? Why, to give the pony his Easter egg, of course. I didn't get one because I'm too old, but the horse did and he's not even a human. I had no idea that equine Easter eggs even existed, but it's just one more thing to stick on the 'nag shit I didn't know' pile, with all the rest.

I have to say, I'm pretty impressed that some enterprising person somewhere has spotted a gap in the market and worked out a way to get horses involved. I mean, the pony must've felt so left out up till now and had to celebrate the resurrection of Jesus in some other, more personal way.

Of course, the whole thing was mainly just an excuse for CC2 to cuddle the pony and allow it to slobber all over her, but he was a little circumspect about the egg and not entirely convinced about the whole thing. He'd take a bite, pull a face, spit some of it out... and then repeat the whole process until he'd eaten it all anyway, which in fairness was much like I did with the poisoned cookie. It might not have been the perfect treat, but he's bright enough not to look a gift human in the mouth.

You'd think that being considered less important than the nag would be bad enough, but at least I get to hold my own as a respected adult member of the family, right? I mean, sure, I get to pay the bills and fix the car and take the bins out, and all the other great stuff that CC1 considers to be a *blue job*, but does CC2 actually listen if I ask her to do something, for example? Well, no, not really, unless I pull out the really big guns and threaten her with that most awful form of child abuse known. Yes, that's right — I'm not proud of it, and I hate myself afterwards when we've all calmed down, but from time to time, when I've really been pushed to the edge and lost my temper, I've felt I had no choice and submitted to the last resort... of turning the wi-fi off. That tends to get the bedroom tidy in record time.

However, even the flimsy fragment of authority that comes with knowing the router password is redundant when we pass from this mortal world and into the World of Nags, and all my powers are rendered useless down at the hotel. Here, all roles are reversed and CC2 becomes the queen of all she surveys. I think it's because we're in her territory, the place where she's experienced and confident, and in her element. My ignorance and apparent ineptitude mean that I become demoted to someone that can just about be trusted to fill a bucket of water if I'm good.

Of course, I try to avoid spending time at the hotel whenever possible. There's just nothing for me there. It's a foreign land of mud and hoses and buckets and animals with bad teeth, and it has no draw for me at all. There was a barbecue down at the hotel recently, and although I tagged along with the CCs, it just wasn't as good as a normal one for me. I like a good barbie as much as the next man and am never happier than when I've got a beer in one hand and some meat on fire in the other, but even this potentially joyous occasion was tempered slightly for me by its proximity to all the nags and piles of horse shit. It's like being invited to a party in a prison or a hot date on an oil rig. Pleasant in principle, but just spoilt slightly by location.

Much of the time when I go, it's just to drop off or pick up CC2, and that's not so bad as I don't have to spend more than a few minutes there. Picking up is the worst of the two, as she's never actually ready when I arrive, of course. She's rarely even visible, to be honest, and usually requires searching for. Normally I'll find her slobbering over some pony or other, nuzzling into its mane and talking to it in nonsensical baby talk. It's minging.

She'll also traipse a load of mud into my nice, clean car, as well as that overpowering smell that she brings back with her. 'Natural Equestrian Musk,' she calls it. 'Horse piss' I call it.

However, more and more recently I've not been let off the hook when it comes to dropping her off, and she starts to assume her role as *The Boss*.

'Uh uh uh! Where do you think you're going?' she'll demand, as I try to slope off back to the car. This is how she talks to me when we're at the nag hotel like I'm the weird, stupid kid in class that requires strict but simple instructions, coupled with a few basic rewards to make sure I don't get too scared and wet myself.

'Now, why don't you go and fill that bucket up for me, hmm?' she'll say, nodding to the tap, while she gets on with the more skilled and grown-up tasks. So I dutifully wander off, dragging my feet as I go, hands stuffed deep into pockets. I'm a grown man with a mortgage and a pension, yet I feel about six when I'm there.

'Oh good boy, well done!' she'll say when I return with the bucket successfully filled. 'Gold star for you!'

Last time, she made me poo pick, and I was not happy about that. I have standards, y'know.

CC2: Right, poo picking next.
Me: No way. No. Uh uh. I'll drive you here, I'll even pay for the damned pony, but I'm not picking up its shit.
CC2: Come come, it'll be over before you realise.
Me: No. I'm not doing it.
CC2: Now don't take that tone with me, young man. Come on!
Me: Well, I'll push the wheelbarrow, but I'm not touching anything brown.
CC2: We'll do it together. It'll take no time.
Me: Fine, but you're doing any sloppy ones. Can we have ice cream afterwards?

Fast forward ten minutes and I'm doing all the picking while she's leaning against a fence checking her social media. She's a slave driver, I tell you. A 14-year-old slave driver with an iPhone. AND I didn't even get ice cream.

This reversal of roles often starts before we even get to the hotel, to be honest. If there are horses in the immediate future, then she kicks into her bossy madam mode and lets nothing get in her way of seeing the pony. I had no garden chores I could do on a recent wet Saturday and decided to take advantage of my empty schedule to fire up the PlayStation and settle in for a nice marathon of virtual shooting, driving and killing. Little did I know that CC1 was also taking it easy and had told CC2 that I would drive her down to the hotel. My study door burst open and CC2 was stood there, literally tapping her feet with arms crossed, wearing a scowl like a 14-year-old Nora Batty as she eyed me up and down.

'Look at you!' she spat with utter contempt. 'A man of your age, playing on a PlayStation in the middle of the morning!'

Meekly trying to defend myself, I countered quickly: 'Oh yeah? So when should I be playing it then?'

'About thirty years ago!' she shot back before walking off to get my car keys for me.

She's got a mean tongue, that young lady.

I look back fondly to those halcyon days of my childhood when adults would ask me what I wanted to be when I grew up. I genuinely believed that I was going to be a jet pilot because, at that age, you don't see any reason why you shouldn't be one. It's a real job, after all, and you see real people on the telly doing it, so it stands to reason that if that's what you choose to do when you're bigger, then there's nothing to stop you.

Of course, when I was seven I didn't know anything about rent, mortgages, relationships, qualifications, job security and all the other myriad elements that factor into your career choices; I just thought that fast planes were pretty cool.

I also didn't know much about the strict entry requirements of the RAF, such as being able to follow rules, get up early, be physically fit, stay sober, and generally not be an idle bastard — all qualities I didn't really possess when I came to be a young adult.

However, I'm not sure how impressed I'd have been if shown what life would entail by the time of my forties. Firstly, nobody tells you about the really bad stuff that happens, like not being able to eat ice cream all day because you'll become morbidly obese, or all that hair that starts growing out of your ears.

I suppose if I had joined the Air Force, then I'd probably be really senior by now. I'd have loads of subordinates calling me 'sir' and jumping at my every command. As it is, I'm made to clear up shit by a 14-year-old and I lose out on all the luxuries in life because a smallish horse gets them instead of me. I never saw all that coming, I can tell you.

I got up at the crack of dawn
To do my garden mowing
I have to do it every week
The bastard grass keeps growing

I worked so hard in my back yard
My old bones were a-creaking
I'd get someone to help me but
It's dear, financially speaking

I had to do it early, see
Appointments we were keeping
We then drove to the yard to wake
The nag who was still sleeping

We took the pony to a spa
Was very nice I'm guessing
I've never been to one myself
Which I find quite depressing

It's not that it appealed to me
In fact it looked quite boring
If I spent ages floating still
I'd probably end up snoring

But even so, forget all that
It's not the point I'm making
I wouldn't mind the option cos
My back is really aching

CHAPTER 2

Stay ignorant. Stay Safe.

STAY IGNORANT. STAY SAFE.

Ten or so years ago, I knew nothing at all about horses. I mean, in the context of large quadrupeds I knew which ones they were, and would've been relatively confident that in some kind of surreal, police line-up with a horse, a cow and maybe even a donkey I'd have been able to identify the nag nine times out of ten, but that was as far as it went. I didn't know anything about how they worked or what they were for, and I'm not even sure I'd ever physically touched one, let alone bought one.

Those were happier times.

These days I'm exposed to horses every day, in one way or other. Even if I don't leave the house to watch CC2 do prancing somewhere, the horseness somehow comes to find me in my own home, like a parking ticket you thought you could get away with by pretending it just 'fell off' the windscreen. There is literally no escape anymore.

Aside from the variety of physical nagaphernalia that litters the house, dinner time at the kitchen table tends to descend into verbal canter banter, eventually. This usually starts when we've all finished eating and we drop into the Phone Zone — that period when we all get our mobiles out so we can look busy, avoid eye contact and hope that someone else will put the dishes away. At this point, either CC1 or CC2 will inevitably find something online that requires sharing with the class, and I get exposed. It could be the results of some international prancing competition, gossip about who's bought or sold some horse or other, or one of a million other dreary, nag-related things.

One common, recurring theme centres around the stacking of clothing onto the ponies. It could be to decide on which matchy matchy colours would be best for the following day's prancing practice, or it could be the rug chat, but layering some kind of fabric onto them is a daily favourite topic. Sometimes I'm asked my opinion on the matchy matchy, but only so I'll be made to look stupid. 'Which colour do you think we should go with tomorrow?' CC2 might ask me, her eyes twinkling with mischief.

'Er... the *Overdraft Orange*?' I'll hazard, warily.

'Orange! On a palomino! Are you quite, quite mad?!'

'Um... *Drainpipe Black* then?'

'Oooh... we don't have a black. Are you buying a black set for us then?'

At this point, I'll back away and, conceding defeat, start to fill the dishwasher.

The rug chat is a popular topic, especially when it's cold outside, which covers about 95% of the year. A weather app will get opened and one of the CCs will declare what temperature it'll be during the night and what's in store for the following day so they can discuss rug strategy at length. As far as I can tell, this is the only benefit of having horse people in the house; it's like having

John Kettley live with us, albeit a John Kettley who's obsessed by nags.

Now, I don't speak *Rug* of course, so I have no idea what they're talking about after the weather itself has been announced, but what I've learned from this nightly conversation is that we own too many rugs and that the nags are spoiled, although I suppose I already knew that second bit. The conversation tends to be something like this:

CC1: Ooh look, it'll be minus 4 tonight!

CC2: Oh no, will it? But I only put a 250 on him!

CC1: The dark blue medium?

CC2: No, you're thinking about the two heavy mediums. This one's red.

CC1: Not the fleecy one?

CC2: No, that's the green 300.

CC1: Ah yes. I was picturing one of the blue lightweight 100 combo indoor/outdoor turnout ones. What's the temperature tomorrow?

Sometimes they don't even use 'celsius' as a measure for temperature, they just talk in degrees of rug. CC2 might look out the window and say 'Looks chilly out there... must be nearly a 300.' Which is no help to me at all and I have to ask for a conversion.

The thing that scares me most about these kinds of conversations is that I'll accidentally learn something about horses. It's bad enough being surrounded by the things and having to pay a fortune to keep them, the last thing I need is any actual knowledge seeping in and corrupting me. My view is that there's a finite amount of storage in the brain and I don't want to waste any of that precious, precious space with useless facts about nags. I need all I've got to store old song lyrics from the 1970s and acceleration times for every model of Ferrari ever made, that kind of thing. You know, useful things.

It's important to keep your guard up at all times, and I've seen what can happen to the unwary. CC1, for example, used to be relatively normal, horse-wise. I think she may have had lessons briefly as a young child, but she escaped relatively unscathed, rejoined society, and went on to live a full and active life as an adult. But CC2's influence has corrupted her totally, and she's now at least as bad in terms of the total hours per day browsing useless, nag-related shit online.

It's like that zombie movie. Doesn't matter which one really, they're all the same. I sometimes feel like I'm one of a handful of survivors, trapped in a dystopian near-future where I'm surrounded by the manky half-dead, clothes torn and covered in hay and horse shit, staggering towards me slowly with arms outstretched, trying to go for my neck... or my wallet. It's hard to tell which sometimes.

If you're someone in my position, trapped in a household of horse people like your own personal *Night of the Living Dead*, then you need to resist. If you start showing any interest, then it's like succumbing to a little nibble, zombie-wise. The nag disease will spread quickly through your body and into your brain, and before you know it, you'll let out a blood-curdling scream and then go online to order matching numbnut and legwarmers in a divine Vet Arm Red with a dead-eyed stare.

So far, I think I've done pretty well, all things considered, and I can say with some pride that I'm really pretty ignorant. Every so often, CC2 will test me on my horse knowledge, knowing full well that she can make me look stupid very easily, and this is a perfectly understandable ambition in any young teenager when dealing with a parent. In most other conversational topics, I'll know more than her, naturally enough. I've been alive for well over three times the amount of time that she has, and it's only to be expected that I've picked up more general knowledge along the way. If we discuss science, capitals of the world, politics, or music up to and including 1998, then she'll have to concede defeat every time, but she has an ace up her sleeve with the nag knowledge, and she loves to wield it.

A case in point was a few months ago when she had a new pony magazine. I've no idea where it came from — like all (the cheaper) horse-related things around the house, it sort of just materialised, so I'm assuming CC1 bought it for her.

From seeing these nag mags in the house over the years, I've deduced that they are arranged across three different tiers: the first kind are on the introductory rung and are aimed at little kids who are new to the wonderful world of ponies. They're called things like 'My Gorgeous Fluffy Ponykins' and are just full of shit photos people have sent in of their little overgrown teddies with bows in their hair. Also 'how to' guides such as 'How to stroke your pony for 8 hours without smothering it to death'.

The second tier is the junior rung for girls who are Big Girls now and well above all that fluffy shit, or at least claim to be. They're called far more serious things like 'My Pony' and are now full of shit photos people have sent in of their steed jumping over poles suspended 1mm above the ground by two strong ants. Also 'how to' guides such as 'How to plait a mane using shiny ribbons'.

The third tier is the senior rung for grown-ups, or

thereabouts, and is no-nonsense. These magazines are simply called things like 'Horse' and are full of shit photos people have sent in of themselves jumping over comedy windmills at eventing events. Also 'how to' guides such as 'How to clean all the disgusting encrusted stuff off your stallion's pony nuts'.

CC2 is still just about at the tier 2 stage and, weirdly, reading them is one of the few things left that she still enjoys doing with me, now that activities such as going anywhere together and conversation are beneath her. Normally, of course, reading would best be conducted in her room, with door shut and music played through the tinny speakers of a phone, just because she knows it'll annoy me and that I'll point out we have a perfectly good stereo downstairs, and generally sound like an old grandad from the 1950s.

But the horse magazine is best enjoyed in my company for two solid reasons. The first is that she can point out all the things she'd like me to buy her... for birthdays, Christmas, or just because it's a Thursday. But the second is, of course, so that she can test me on my horse knowledge and therefore belittle me as much as possible. It's like her two favourite hobbies combined into one.

The magazine will normally have at least one quiz of some kind, but she doesn't stop there and will casually flip through the pages before seeing something suitably well out of my sphere of knowledge and demand an answer to a made-up question. 'What brand of hat is that?' she demanded last time, pointing to a photo of someone in the far distance, possibly riding a horse. 'Oh... er... Sam Gatehouse? Er... KAP? Er... Benson & Hedges? PJ & Duncan?'

She looked at me with a mixture of pity and disgust. 'No, it's a Charles Owen,' she declared haughtily.

'Oh. Isn't he an actor?'

Pity, disgust and confusion.

A few pages on, she found an advert for some horse rug, covered the price with her hand and asked me how much it would cost.

'Er... a hundred thousand pounds?' I ventured.

'No,' she sneered, 'it's not even a winter rug, it's only a lightweight technomesh 250 neoprene performance rug with a liquid centre.'

'Oh, right. Er... TWO hundred thousand then?'

She just grunted and flicked to the next page with an immense amount of disdain.

But then we came to a quiz and her little eyes lit up. Now she could not only embarrass me but accurately score my level of ignorance and inadequacy to the nearest point.

'Right!' she announced, 'If you get more than half of these right you don't have to buy me that new matchy matchy set in MasterCard Mauve.'

'But I don't have to anyway!' I shot back with a little bit of high-pitched desperation in my voice.

'Oh yes you do-hooo!' she sang without even looking up at me.

So, first question with everything to play for. 'Which month are the Burghley horse trials held? September, October or November?'

Oh bollocks, how the fuck am I supposed to know that? I picked a random month; September. She didn't answer, but by the grunt she made under her breath as she looked back down at the page, I assume I guessed right.

Next question. 'Where do you measure a horse's height from?'

'Easy — the ground!' Nothing, not even a flicker of a smile. Wrong. One out of two.

'Which horse did Charlotte of the Garden ride to her bronze medal at the World Equestrian Games?'

'Well, Valegro, of course. It's always Valegro.'

Wrong! A different horse entirely, apparently, Mount St George or something. Who knew? So she has two horses, eh? Pretty flash.

And so it went on. I'm afraid to say that I was tested and found wanting. And CC2 savoured every last delicious drop of my defeat with the sort of unbridled pleasure she usually reserves for butterscotch Angel Delight.

Realising she could probably embarrass me even further still, she then managed to find something else to test me on, so my ordeal wasn't over yet. There was a picture of a horse with arrows pointing to all its bits that you had to name and write down in little boxes. There were clues provided, but she carefully scribbled over them all with a Sharpie, just to make sure that my next crushing defeat was guaranteed.

Now, this one was both easier and harder in that some bits were obvious, even to a complete nagtard like me. It started off slowly, and I got "ears" successfully. Yay, go me! After that it went quickly downhill, I'm sorry to admit. There were just arrows everywhere, pointing at the bits of space between the recognisable actual bits.

'Err... the top? No? "Back" then?' Apparently not specific enough, it was "withers". Next bit. 'Erm... bum? No? Rear? Oooh, how about rump? Oh no, that's a steak.' It was "dock" apparently. WTF?

I was pretty pleased with myself that I got "fetlock", mind you. Though when I say 'I got' fetlock, I just mean I got the word right. Turns out I was about as far away as possible from being right and thought it was on the head. Stupid me! Stupid, ignorant, useless me!

The rest of the words I'd never even heard of. Except for elbow, of course, which is in completely the wrong place, by the way. If your elbow is next to your knee, then you've been in a very nasty accident. No wonder the long face. I may not know my equine arse from my elbow, but it turns out that nobody else does either.

So I failed miserably and consequently 'owed' her a matchy matchy set by way of recompense. I've no idea how that was supposed to work, but don't worry — on top of being a complete failure at naming horse parts, I also disappointed her further by showing her how to welch on a deal... "Deal" being very much in air quotes.

In a way, we both got something out of the hour. I got the closest approximation to quality time that I get with her these days, and she got to grind my face into the ground, metaphorically speaking, and prove that I'm a pointless and ignorant old man. Win/win. I guess.

I have to admit, though, I've shown worse ignorance before that was even more damning in her eyes. Admittedly, it wasn't being scored this time, but I think she was actually a little shocked by how much I really don't know.

I was dropping her off at the nag hotel, as is fairly standard. And so far, so good, I managed that perfectly well enough and nobody died. She wandered off and was chatting to her trainer, so I thought I'd go and say hello to the nag as it was a nice day and I didn't relish sitting in the car waiting for hours. Now, as you've probably guessed, I don't spend an awful lot of time with the nags generally. I don't have the kind of relationship with them that CC2 does, which, as far as I can tell, is some weird kind of human/equine love affair. There's lots of stroking and nuzzling and they not only spend time practising and training but go on endless long country walks together. It makes no sense to me at all. To me, the nag is like a gigantic, hairy piggy bank that I drop money into every day, but one that only accepts credit cards, cheques and higher-denomination banknotes. No crappy fivers or coins for this little piggy.

However, much as I like to blame it for my crappy car, lack of holidays, threadbare carpet, Brexit and climate change, I have to concede that it's just an innocent bystander in many ways and didn't ask for any of this. Sure, it gets board and lodging all paid for, good meals and regular haircuts, but it also gets roused early in the morning when it'd rather be sleeping still and made to walk up and down an empty horse pitch for no discernible reason. It's very similar to being in the army when you think about it, except the uniform is more colourful and there are fewer guns. But it didn't even sign up for anything voluntarily, it's just a kind of dressage conscript. We're in the same boat to some degree, though I'm not sure I like the idea of being in a boat with him; very high centre of gravity, horses.

So I wandered over to go and say hello to it, and as he poked his head out over the door, I rather fancied he recognised me and gave me a 'hello' in the form of a disgusting little snort.

I gave it a stroke down the front of its long, bony face in the safe area that's between the eye bit and the mouth bit, and I felt we bonded that little bit more. It even did a sort of nag smile and showed me his rancid yellow teeth, which was nice. Yep, I thought, he definitely likes me, maybe even knows on some level that I'm his benefactor and that he should be grateful to me. We had a little chat, though I was polite enough to keep the conversation away from money, and I concluded that perhaps the nag was ok after all and that I should spend a bit more time being nice to it.

My reverie was broken by a shout from behind me — 'Oi, over here!' I turned to see CC2 and her trainer standing by a different stable and stroking a brown horse poking out of that one. 'It's this one, dummy,' CC2 continued to shout at me, 'we moved him last week.'

As I said, I can just about tell the difference between a horse and a cow, but after that, I can't promise anything and they sort of blur into one. They're all brown and horse-shaped, after all.

During prancing lessons, I get to hear a lot of detailed instruction shouted by the trainer, and I can tell you with all honesty that I understand nothing at all that's said. I mean, sure, I understand the individual words, but they're used in sentences that are baffling to me. The thing that I'm still genuinely unconvinced by is whether anyone else actually understands what's being said either, as the commands are seemingly made up on the spot and don't appear to relate to anything I'm looking at in any way. I'll be watching a young girl, sat on a horse and trotting along happily, and the trainer will bark bizarre things like 'Hold him from the tent pole! Tighten the underbelly and stop him from swinging the rabbit so much on the left side!'

At this, I'll twist my head towards CC2, eyes narrowed, to see what she does differently, and can never detect any change at all. She'll just carry on in exactly the same way as before. 'Good!' the trainer will shout encouragingly, 'That's better! Can you feel how he's now looser around the centre-shaft and not pulling on the teapot so much?'

Brow now deeply furrowed in suspicion, I'll swing back to CC2, who'll be nodding earnestly as if they've really all turned a corner together. It's clearly a wind-up, and I suspect that CC2 just agrees with anything she's asked in order to keep everyone happy.

CC1 is often there as well, and she and the trainer will exchange nag chat knowingly too.

'Look at his canter!' CC1 said recently.
'It's a great canter,' the trainer agreed.
'Amazing canter.'
'It's a really good canter, definitely.'

Pause

'It's a really good canter.'
'Oh, great canter.'

Pause

'Great strides.'
'Really good strides.'

Pause

'Great canter.'
'Really nice canter.'

It's all bollocks, I'm telling you. If I've accidentally learnt anything at all over the last few years, it's that the nag's got a really good canter, which either includes, or is the same as, 'strides'.

I have to confess that I did actually learn a genuine

horse fact recently, though, and I was very unhappy about it. I never mean to learn anything, you understand, it's just that sometimes some sort of nag-related fact gets through my barriers, into my ears and then slowly, by osmosis, into my brain against my will. It's like when a rebellious child who's sat at the back of a maths class with his fingers in his ears singing 'la-la-la' relaxes for a second to take a breath and some algebra accidentally gets in.

You see, I was watching with rapt fascination as CC2 and a whole load of other horse people rode around in endless dreary circles for fourteen hours straight, and every few moments one of the nags would trot past where I was standing. A couple of them were making that leathery squeaking sound as one bit of tack somewhere was presumably rubbing on some other bit in time to the trot, so I asked CC1 about it, more to pass the time than out of any genuine curiosity.

'What's rubbing on what to make that sound?' I asked through a stifled yawn. 'Is it the saddle or the boots, I can't quite make it out.'

'Er, no,' she said, looking at me in a mildly amused and slightly quizzical way. I knew something weird was about to happen. 'That's the sound of the sheath as air's expelled.'

I looked at her for a full three seconds and blinked. 'I'm sorry, that's the what now?'

'The sheath. The foreskin. It's only the boy horses that do it.'

I didn't say anything this time. I just squinted at her sideways.

CC1 laughed and continued. 'As their muscles tense when they trot, it forces air out, and the sheath makes that sound. It's quite an odd noise, isn't it?'

I just carried on looking at her in silence, unsure of what to say. I felt very much like I did at the age of seven when I discovered that babies don't actually come out of the belly button at all, but out of a lady's foo-foo. Once you learn these things, there's no going back to the not-knowing of just a few moments before. That innocence is lost forever.

I turned back to watch the nags as they trotted past. 'Fwerp, fwerp, fwerp, fwerp,' went one of the boy horses.

I looked back at CC1, who was watching me with poorly disguised amusement.

'Seriously?'

'Yes. Seriously.'

I paused to take it all in. 'I want to go home now, please.'

Steve Jobs, the founder of Apple, famously used the phrase 'Stay hungry. Stay foolish.' as a way of encouraging an attitude of passionate and experimental enthusiasm in young entrepreneurs. That's all very well if you're setting out to build a tech company, but what if you're living with a load of nag zombies who insist on filling both the house and all conversation with horse-related shit? To be honest, I can kind of relate to the 'stay hungry' bit, but more in the sense of not being able to afford food anymore, rather than in being ambitious.

For those in my position, though, I would suggest a different slogan that it might be useful to adhere to: *Stay ignorant. Stay safe*. It might not make you rich, but just as in all the zombie movies, it's the coming out alive at the end of the day that's the most important thing. Ideally with your brain intact, even if not your wallet.

'A little knowledge is a dangerous thing'
I learnt one day in school
So I stopped listening from that point
To dodge being made a fool

If teacher handed me a book
I'd say 'Oh, no thanks, Miss!'
'I've got no time for that today'
Cos ignorance is bliss

CHAPTER 3

Don't get too attached to your money

DON'T GET TOO ATTACHED TO YOUR MONEY

Here's a question for you: is it expensive to live with a horse person? Now, if you're yet to enter the world of nags and are reading this book for the purposes of research, then you may find yourself leaning forward in your seat and adjusting your glasses at this point, keen to learn the answer. If however, you're a horse person already, then you've probably just scoffed out loud with a Mrs Krabappel-style 'Ha!', and possibly even wiped tears of mirth from your eyes... assuming you can still afford tears. I'll cut to the chase here — yes, horses are expensive to own and keep. Not a little bit spendy, either, like a few twenties here and there and the odd big purchase of a couple of grand, but properly spendy, in a sort 'how many times can you mortgage the house' Google search history kind of way.

What we're dealing with is the world of *Naganomics* — the finances connected with all things equine — and it's generally not a very pretty world. My own experience indicates that the expenses just keep getting more expensive, which is unfortunate because I keep getting poorer. This doesn't bode well for the future, when you think about it; the maths isn't looking good.

It doesn't matter whether a horse is young or old, active, lazy, big, small, fat or thin, their very existence is charged by the hour. They need hotel rooms, food, rigging, clothing, vet's fees, insurance, rugs, supplements, shoes, cleaning, brushing, saddles, salt, physios, chiropractors, masseurs, slaves, asses' milk etc etc etc. And this is before you do anything at all with them like actually ride the thing or chauffeur them around in a massive fucking lorry.

Have you ever watched Formula 1? You know how the teams arrive in vast transporters, unload their 20-million-pound cars and then have hundreds of people fussing around them, five at each wheel, ten studying the computer screens and endless others whose job it is to be responsible for a particular bolt or piece of bodywork? Well, it's no coincidence that the Ferrari badge has a horse on it, that's all I'm saying. You might have the urge to put on some protective clothing and a nice expensive helmet, then wait in a chair while everyone gets everything ready, but that shit ain't cheap.

In my previous book, there was a chapter entitled 'Are horses expensive?', in which I discussed the basic costs of buying horses and saddles, and all the other predictably necessary stuff. We can skip over that here or else you might just think that the two books are essentially the same, which is ridiculous, but I think we can assume that the start-up costs of getting a horse and putting it up in a hotel indefinitely are not insignificant.

The problem with horse people, though, is that they don't know when to stop. Owning a horse isn't so much a hobby or a sport as a lifestyle choice, and there appears to be no stage at which they have all the things they require to ride, the purchasing phase is complete, and they're able to stop buying things. Our house is like some kind of distribution centre for nag-related crap, albeit in reverse.

Back when I was a kid, we used to get proper post. By which I mean letters and shit, you know, things that people would write to each other as a form of communication. Since email, that's all pretty much died off. If I see actual handwriting on the front of an envelope in our post pile, I just assume our dog's bitten a neighbour again and they've written another angry note. We still get post, of course, more of it than ever in fact. A lot of it is bills and bank statements — the former going into detail about why the latter is so depressing.

What a lot of our post has in common these days is having a little image of a horse on it somewhere, or being sent from a company called 'Equi-something'. It could be a catalogue of matchy matchy shit, it could be paperwork of some kind or, most likely, it could be a bill. Insurance, vet fees, farriers, that kind of thing. They won't be addressed to me usually but I'll know anyway because the return-to address on the back will say 'Equicare', 'Equivet' or 'Equishoe', guaranteed. The matchy catalogues usually come in transparent plastic so I can spot their gaudy numbnuts a mile off, and sneak them into the recycling bin before anyone else gets to see them.

We also seem to receive a lot of parcels, similarly named and stamped with pictures of horses. I don't usually know what's in these, but I assume they're clothes either for the horse or for CC2 to wear while sitting on a horse. I just know that I've probably paid for them, despite them not being sent to me. A parcel arrived recently that was actually addressed to me, clearly sent from a purveyor of nag wear. Knowing full well that I'd ordered no such thing,

I concluded that CC1 has given up even trying to conceal the fact that she's using my bank card to buy all this shit. She couldn't even be arsed to put her own name on the order this time.

Naturally, I opened it anyway, out of principle. I'm sure I read once that if you open someone else's mail, then you get sent to the Tower of London by the Queen, although that might be if you kill a swan. I don't know why anyone would kill a swan, mind you, unless it was in self-defence; they're quite bitey when you get too close to them and can break your arm with their wings, y'know. But anyway, there's no rule against opening your own post, even if you know it's not intended for you. So, I excitedly ripped it open just because I could, trying to pretend it'd be something good, but of course, it was just some awful child-sized jodhpurs, as I knew deep down that it probably would be.

I left the ripped-open packaging on the kitchen table, as a clear warning to both the CCs that I'll definitely open anything addressed to me, however nag-related it clearly is. If I pay, then I open! I'm not sure what to do about the jodhpurs though. They're tight as fuck and look a bit stupid with my leather jacket, but presumably they'll stretch?

It's even worse if the two CCs go to any kind of big prancing event, as they probably feel safer out of my sight, and I know from bitter experience that wherever horses congregate in large enough numbers, someone will build a shop. If the event is important enough, then they sometimes have video live-streamed onto some website or obscure TV channel, and I can watch this from the comfort of my sofa. I have no interest in the nags, of course, but I like to see if I can spot the CCs spending any money. If I sit close enough to the TV, I can try to find them in the crowd and identify any new garments I don't recognise that they've picked up there. They usually come home from these things hiding shopping bags behind them, CC2 rushing straight up to her bedroom guiltily, so it's best to just catch them in the act if possible.

I actually dual-screen while I'm watching — I can perch my iPad next to the TV and have it showing my bank account. These instant transactions nowadays are amazing and I can fire off a questioning text to CC1 within 30 seconds of a purchase. She normally just claims it's lunch, something to do with cheesy chips usually, but I can't really believe they can spend £120 on chips, however deliciously cheesy they are.

The very worst event of all is some big thing they have annually at the Olympia Centre in London, and this is a firm date in the CCs' calendar. I don't fully understand what it is, but it seems to be some kind of combination of horse event and shopping. I'm not sure which is the priority and whether you shop in between watching horses or watch horses in between shopping, but either way, it's the CCs' earthly approximation of heaven. As I understand it, some of the best prancers in the land walk up and down and go in circles as the crowd goes wild, so it's a particular treat for CC2, who gets to watch her heroes work their magic at close range.

The fact that this thing is always scheduled just before Christmas makes it a particularly dangerous event, financially speaking, and I get very nervous and sweaty in the days leading up to it. I like to spend some quality time with any money I still have at this stage and curl up on the sofa with it while we open a bottle of wine and watch a rom-com together.

I think CC1 sees it as a kind of end-of-year book-keeping exercise. In her mind, once the bills and mortgage have been taken care of and we get to December, then anything I still have rattling around in the bottom of my bank account can rightfully be spent on whatever horse-related tat she likes. It makes the books balance nicely in her eyes and does me a favour. All I know is that they come back late, staggering wearily up the driveway, leaning forward at 45 degrees while dragging 18 bags each behind them, like a really shit event in a World's Strongest Woman competition. Except held at night and on my driveway. And hauling loads of soft, pink cotton products instead of tractor wheels or 747s.

Last year, I thought that my presence might moderate the spending, so I suggested that I come along with them to make it a nice family day out. This was met with icy silence over the dinner table, forks frozen in mid-air as the CCs locked eyes with each other. CC2 calmly put her fork down, patted her mouth with a napkin, cleared her throat and said, slowly, 'Well... you can come, but you have to stay silent during the shows. One word and you're out.'

Frankly, this moment of pint-sized, Godfather-esque intimidation put the willies up me a bit. I had visions of accidentally speaking during a particularly gripping 20-metre circle and then waking up the next morning to find my decapitated motorcycle lying next to me, my hands slick with freshly spilt engine oil.

On top of this, CC1 pointed out that it goes on all day and ends at about 3 in the morning, and not even on the same day you got there. 'Are you sure you want to spend 164 hours looking at horses and horse stuff?' she asked.

I've been to Olympia a few times myself over the years, but usually for the annual beer festival. The entire, vast building, stuffed wall-to-wall with an endless range of lovely, lovely beers from around the world. *Gurgle*. You start off the morning making considered choices as to what to try, based on geographic region, style of beer and cost. Come the early afternoon, you're making less wise decisions, by late afternoon making frankly reckless decisions and by the evening making decisions that you later have no recollection of whatsoever. I think I've been three times, but I can't be sure.

I made a mental image of all the beer being replaced with matchy matchy shit, rigging, sparkly horse tiaras and rugs and decided, on balance, that maybe I didn't want to go after all and left them to attend alone, as usual.

If there are no nag events to go to and no 'necessary' purchases such as saddles and numbnuts to be made, then both the CCs are perfectly capable of making up reasons to buy things, anyway. Sometimes it takes creative thinking to come up with an angle, but never let it be said that either of them lacks creativity when it comes to buying things for the horse, for CC2 while on the horse, or for any other situation that can somehow be connected to the horse with enough effort.

There is a series of purchases I like to call 'Nag-Related Things That We Apparently Need To Buy To Solve A Problem I Didn't Even Know Existed,' or NRTTWANTBTSAPIDEKE for short. Some of the more fondly remembered entries in this series have been #134 - *A Hay Steamer*, #46 - *Eight Metric Tons of Salt*, #103 - *A Different Kind of Saddle* and of course, my least favourite of all, #1 - *A Horse*.

#172 was A Wireless Intercom System, and it was a classic move by CC1 to try and persuade me to buy something that had no real purpose whatsoever. The 'problem' she posited was as follows:

While having lessons and warming up before prancing competitions, CC2 needed to be able to better hear the instructions and ministrations of her trainer while she repeatedly says 'Hands!' to her.

Now, I'm perfectly comfortable with the concept of trainer and trainee being able to communicate with each other. I pay handsomely for the services of the trainer and wouldn't want to think she just stands around watching CC2 circle her for no particular reason, her head lolling at 45 degrees purely out of boredom, or an oddly heavy head.

I thought back to when I was a child, going to football practice on Saturday mornings. We were equally instructed vocally by a (much cheaper BTW) football coach, but, as I recall, he wasn't decked out like Tom Cruise in an endlessly franchised action spy movie, with a high-tech Bluetooth earpiece to whisper tense instructions. No. He was a fat bloke in a nylon tracksuit who used to shout at us.

So why can't CC2's trainer just raise her voice? It's not like she's stationed in a secret underground headquarters while CC2 and the nag attempt to avoid laser sensors on the other side of the city by doing an evasive 10-metre circle. No, she's usually just over there, look. About 30 feet away, tops, standing on the same horse pitch.

I posed this question to CC1, in response to the web links she was texting me to multi-million-pound headsets. And the answer was apparently that, during warmups for competitions, everybody else on the practice pitch can hear the trainer's guidance and can take advantage of it.

Is that really what it's like? Does everyone 'steal' advice in earshot? I was then visualising a pitch full of girls on nags, all riding around as quietly as possible like comedy burglars passing a window, their heads craning to hear the valuable nuggets of wisdom being issued by CC2's trainer. Every time she shouted out something like, 'OK, let's try a 20-metre circle', the whole amassed group of riders would suddenly start to turn in perfect unison, as if by complete coincidence, while the trainer narrowed her eyes in suspicion.

I looked into these headsets, of course, and they do exist. They're a ton of money for normal people doing normal things, and then also available with an added 100% Horse Tax for the 'equine version' that comes in pink with a horseshoe logo on the box. Naganomics, you see.

In this particular instance, I had to put my foot down and I vetoed the purchase, but being a generous chap, I tried to come up with my own solution as a compromise, utilising things we already own. I started off with some old tin cans and a long length of string, but that had practical difficulties and we ended up playing Cat's Cradle with the nag. But with a bit more thinking, I was able to come up with a winner...

On modern mobile phones, there's a mode for the hearing impaired whereby it amplifies sound it picks up and then plays it through headphones. I think it's designed for people watching TV and things; you sit your phone on the arm of your chair with the microphone pointing to the telly, pop some headphones on and it magnifies the sound. Perfect!

So, all we had to do was to duct-tape CC2's phone around her head and plug in some headphones. It wasn't quite 'Mission: Impossible 27 - Enter at A', but it did the trick and the pony didn't get tied up in a knot. Sometimes creative ways to spend money can be countered with creative ways not to.

CC2 is also perfectly capable of trying to fill any non-horse-shaped holes in her life with horse-shaped purchases, and her birthday and Christmas lists tend to be prime examples of the lateral thinking she employs in her retail lust. She's able at will to reel off a string of items that I didn't even know existed, but that somehow fill a void in the nag world with great imagination. Take, for example, new trainers. Aha, you're thinking, they aren't even horsey, they're just shoes, right? Wrong.

Firstly, the specific ones she wanted are made by a very popular brand of horse-related tat ('The Gucci of horse clothing', CC2 told me) and they have only one planned role in life. They're specifically to be worn at prancing shows, after the riding itself is over and the boots have been removed but designed to look good with jodhpurs. They're for making a statement. A sort of casual, 'Yeah, I was just riding — but now I'm not. No big deal' kind of thing. Shoes for wearing between horse boots and normal shoes, like a sort of 'come-down' shoe, or an airlock between an equine version of a deep-sea dive and dry land. Footwear to match rosettes if you will, but basically just for showing off in. In other words, they're just normal trainers, albeit overpriced in line with the brand name on them that's associated with other stuff the company also makes that's well respected... but that isn't actually these.

Another present she got for her last birthday was a candle. Aha, you're thinking again, a perfectly normal, not-at-all horsey item. And it would be too if it weren't scented to smell like hay. Yes, that's right, you can buy candles designed to smell like a manky old stable. It seems a little odd to me to mix the concepts of dried grass and naked flames, but somebody has and they apparently get on like a house on fire. CC2 opened the lid, drew in a massive breath with eyes screwed up tightly, and let out the most satisfied sigh of contentment I've ever heard. I had a quick whiff myself and was nearly sick. It really does smell like a manky old stable. I think our noses have started to work differently.

Quite why she needs a candle to make her room smell like stale hay and horse piss is anyone's guess, as that's all it ever smells of, anyway, but she seemed happy enough, and who am I to argue? I might try to find one for me called 'Old pub' that reeks of sticky carpets and stale beer. Actually, that does sound pretty good, *goes off to google it*...

It should be obvious, however, that CC2 doesn't require a birthday or Christmas to think about nag-related things she'd like me to buy for her. I think that in her mind, receiving presents on birthdays and Christmases is a bit like women proposing to men on February 29th in leap years — sort of nice to have a special day for it, but a bit limiting and old-fashioned, and a terrible waste of all the other possible opportunities.

She's come up with an alarming new phrase recently, one that's begun to strike fear into my soul whenever I hear it. It's 'I've been thinking...' usually said in a slow, sing-song kind of way, and usually completely out of the blue as she enters the room, presumably as a result of her actually doing some serious thinking somewhere else, and then coming to sound me out about it. What comes next in the sentence is varied, but let me tell you this, it's never anything like '...I should start helping out with the housework more often,' or '...I've decided to start going to bed on time without an argument.'

No. I'll give you a typical example of how these sentences usually pan out:

CC2: I've been thinking...

Me: Oh God.

CC2: I've noticed that the number of likes I get on Instagram posts depends on the quality of the matchy matchy in the photo.

Me: Does it now?

CC2: It does. So, I'm prepared to let you buy me a new set in Gullible Green.

Me: How very generous of you.

CC2: I know, right? And what's more, although we'll be needing the numbnut and bandages and base layers for me, I'm prepared to forgo the fly mask and hat silk.

Me: Hang on... base layers for you?

CC2: Yes.

Me: Matchy matchy shit now extends to clothes for humans too, to match the nag?

CC2: Well, durr!

Me: Oh God.

CC2: And what's more, it's occurred to me, of course, that when it gets colder, I'll be needing a coat and that will cover up my matchy.

Me: Okaaaay...

CC2: And coats are expensive, I realise that. So, as a special favour, I'll let you buy me a body warmer instead. It's like a Friends & Family discount.

Me: Thank you so much.

CC2: You're very welcome.

Me: So let me get this straight... you're going to allow me to buy you a new matchy set, including matching body warmer, but will forgo the fly mask and hat silk?

CC2: I will. It's an incredible offer, one time only, not to be repeated.

Me: But aren't deals supposed to be a two-way thing?

CC2: I suppose.

Me: So...?

CC2: So jump to it!

Me: Not really what I meant. What's in it for me?

CC2: Well, you have a choice.

Me: Oh, cool. What are my options?

CC2: Cash or bank transfer.

I've heard sentences start with 'I've been thinking...' rather a lot lately. They've outlined the logic that would lead me to buying her matchy matchy, buying her a horse ('But you've got a horse'... 'No, that's a pony'), booking tickets to Budapest for some nag event or other ('Be quick! They're currently a bargain!') and me buying next door's field and building an arena on it ('Think of all the money you'll save!'). You can probably spot a pattern.

Last week she accosted me while I was doing the washing up: 'I've been thinking... you need to pull your finger out, I've decided I want to be rich.'

As you can see, I'm a very disappointing parent for her. She's still annoyed with me for refusing to sell my car for horse feed, arguing that I'm barely using it currently. Sadly, she's past that age where she doesn't understand the value of things and I can just tell her the car cost a fiver. Instead, she's more likely now to bring up the online configurator and start working out how much I could've saved on a cheaper model — 'I hope you didn't spec the heated seats, that's a new set of boots right there!'

From time to time, CC1 actually sells some of the accumulated horse crap and this ought to be a positive and joyous occasion with cash doing the opposite of usual and finally coming into the house, like a money salmon swimming upstream on the river of retail, if you will. Now, in most financial areas, you have the concept of money that comes in and money that goes out. In relation to your bank account, for example, wages come in and then bills go out. If the first number is bigger than the second, then this is called 'having money'. I remember this from before I met CC1, but the details are hazy now.

I'm more familiar these days with the second number being the bigger one, and this is when you're introduced to an array of further financial concepts, like 'overdrafts' and 'loans'. It's less nice on the whole, but the bank does tend to write to you more often, so that part makes you feel a little warm inside, if you're desperate.

But then there's the concept of the 'Nag Fund', which is a branch of Naganomics, and this seems to work in a wholly different way. It doesn't appear to go in two directions at all, but just the one. Money goes in and... well, that's it. It just goes in, never to be seen again, no matter what happens.

This week, for example, I found a large lump of leather and metal clogging up the kitchen. 'What's that?' I asked, pointing with arm outstretched and eyes narrowed.

'It's a saddle,' replied CC1. Every day's a school day for me.

'It looks expensive,' I said sadly, 'did I buy it?'

'Yes, you did!' she said. 'A while ago now. Thanks!'

'Right. Sure,' I said and sat down to open the letters from the bank.

CC1 then informed me she was going to be off out soon to buy a new saddle. I looked at her, then at the lump of leather and metal, and then back at her again. I may have pointed again, possibly at both of them in turn.

'But... you have a saddle,' I said weakly.

'Yes, but we need a new one and I've found a bargain for sale. It's only a hundred thousand pounds.' (I can't remember the exact numbers, but you get the idea).

'Wow. Such a bargain. So what's happening to this one then?'

'It's up for sale.'

'Oh. Ok. Good,' I said, grateful that we weren't just collecting saddles for no reason. 'How much are we selling it for?'

'Two hundred thousand pounds!'

'Oh, right,' I said, my mood lifting. 'Cool! So I'll be getting a hundred thousand pounds back then?'

There was a bit of silence at this point. Then eventually some laughter.

'Er, no,' she said simply, with one of those patronising smiles she gives when she catches me browsing Autotrader.

'But... why?' I asked, possibly in a slightly more whiny voice than I'd planned.

'Because we need it. We need to buy some boots.'

Money goes into the Nag Fund, you see, but can never be allowed to escape again. It's like a financial black hole, and any cash that gets anywhere near it will be sucked inside, never to be seen again, possibly spat out into another dimension through the curvature of spacetime, though probably just spent on matchy matchy shit.

This is the essentials of Naganomics as a whole, and anyone that enters the nag world should start thinking of money in the same way that a prison guard thinks about inmates on death row — best not to get too attached, it'll only end up being upsetting eventually.

You might think that the horsey bills
Are food and vet and stable
You might think that it all ends there
That the cards are on the table

Well let me tell you now, my friend
As well as I am able
There's a million other things to buy
With a nag sketch on the label

You can go to the shops with a list that's small
And you'll leave with a bag that's six foot tall
If you don't put a cap on your own indulging
You'll be crushed by the haul with your biceps bulging

CHAPTER 4

Never let a horse onto your property

NEVER LET A HORSE ONTO YOUR PROPERTY

I don't know what you and your significant other like to do in your free time (and nor, indeed, do I wish to find out), but CC1 and I have a favourite game we often play together if we've really run out of things to watch on TV or bicker about. I daresay it's one that you may have played yourselves, and although hitherto untitled, it's essentially the 'What Will We Buy When We FINALLY Win The Bastard Lottery And Become Stinking Rich' game.

For starters, I like to list every car I'll buy for my multi-level, underground garage and if left unchecked for too long can end up spending a considerable amount of time in online configurators, agonising in deep ecstasy over whether my future Aston Martin will have stitching to match the seat leather or perhaps in a contrasting colour to match the roof lining. And don't get me started on the arguments for and against the *20" Lightweight Forged Wheel* versus the *Diamond Turned 21"* option. I've been there, sister, believe me. Naturally, money is no object, so all the extras get ticked off as a matter of principle, except of course the one for the seats which memorise multiple positions for different drivers because THERE'D BE NO POINT. Ha!

CC1 doesn't like the car portion of this game so much, and starts threatening to go and watch *Eastenders* if I start talking about ceramic brakes (very expensive, though probably worth having), but she does like the bit where we look for a house to buy. We fire up the *Rightmove* app, choose a suitably aspirational area and then damned well order the results from most expensive downwards as if money is merely a problem for the accounting staff to deal with.

We sort of agree on various aspects of our future mansion/castle, such as indoor pool, sweeping, tree-lined driveway and enough rooms that we can avoid each other for days at a time. We also each have personal requirements that the other doesn't really care about as long as we get our own stuff as well. She doesn't much care how big my wine cellar will be, for example, or how many lanes the bowling alley will need, as long as she gets a walled herb garden that she can tend to in a big, floppy hat, and an orangery to doze in before we take cocktails on the veranda of an evening.

However, we do disagree on one vital point when perusing and planning our obscenely rich future, and that's whether there needs to be 'equine facilities'. In her mind, no country pile is complete without its own 5-star nag hotel, including oak-framed indoor school and vast acreages of estate-fenced paddocks, ideally on limestone, apparently. 'Think of the money we'd save in livery costs,' she'll say brightly, sort of missing the point in several key ways.

My view on the matter is that my dream house is one

without horses anywhere near it, messing up the place and generally lowering the tone. Plus, my helicopters are bound to scare them, so I'm being thoughtful too. The basic deal between CC1 and me regarding nags goes like this: here, take all my money but leave me enough for petrol and wine, and then take CC2 over there somewhere and do horse stuff together. I don't much care where that 'somewhere' is, but in my mind, it ought at least to be 'somewhere else', and not just next door. I do appreciate that all the driving back and forth for lessons, feeding and shitpicking mean that proximity is a factor, so I have no problem with the hotel being relatively nearby for convenience, but I think there should be an element of separation. Let's say it's one mile as a minimum.

Now, I feel I should mention at this point that we actually have a small paddock at the end of our garden and a little stable at the end of that. I'm not looking for any sympathy at this stage, by the way, I appreciate that it's a bit fancy to have our own stable and wouldn't normally bring it up, but, well, clearly it's relevant. Also, it was here when we moved in, unused, unloved and hidden under a mountain of nettles and thistles; I didn't even know about it until I got the strimmer out.

To be honest, when talking to work colleagues and casual acquaintances, I'd never dream of mentioning the stable, but that's mainly because they might think I like horses. I'd have to lie to save face and make up some less embarrassing purpose for it, such as a sex dungeon or somewhere to store the bodies.

Being small and a bit run-down, neither the stable nor paddock is really suitable for permanent nag residency, and we ended up just sticking a few chickens in there to make some use of it, which meant that we lived on nothing but omelettes for a couple of years. However, there was a point in the past where the CCs managed to sneak a nag in, so I do have some experience of having horses actually live at home with us. And it's terrible.

Firstly, when a nag comes to stay, it doesn't just bring a toothbrush and a change of clothes. Oh no, It's a lot worse than that. Bales of hay, straw, tubs of salt, spray bottles of stuff, brushes, more hay, shitpicking implements, clothes, rugs, clothes, rugs, more salt, buckets etc, etc, etc. They have more possessions than I do. There's nothing casual about a horse coming to stay, it's like a military operation. And by that, I don't mean it's disciplined and executed with precision; I mean there's a convoy of lorries carrying equipment and a lot of shouting.

On top of this, the visit was promised to be very brief and was specifically because they were moving from one nag hotel to another. 'It'll just be a day or two while we find a new yard, honest,' are words that I've come to learn are as dishonest as 'It's not you, it's me.' I should probably have been warned by the amount of equipment that turned up, I suppose. It's like when an elderly relative comes 'for a few days' over Christmas, and then by about June you belatedly appreciate the significance of the massive suitcase they brought, realise that they're clearly not going anywhere and now, apparently, live with you. Until they die.

Of course, the CCs just adored having the pony so close by and I suspect they did everything they could to extend this visit for as long as possible. CC1 appreciated not having to drive back and forth to the hotel each day, and CC2 essentially had the world's largest pet to play with. She spent every waking moment down at the end of the garden, not just to do horse-related things, but to be close to her beloved. This even extended to doing her homework there, sat on the floor, in the wood shavings, books balanced on her crossed legs while the horse helped her with her geography, or any necessary dribble. You might think that it's ever so sweet, but I think it's a little bit disgusting, sat in the pissy bedding. This is where horse people and I differ.

That said, if she ever becomes the new Charlotte of the Garden as she wants to be, and has a movie made about her rise to Olympic glory, it'll definitely be a scene early on in the film. Probably the bit where the star reveals her innermost feelings to the audience by talking to herself or a nearby animal, usually after the big plot setback.

'We'll never make the Olympics now, Fireflash, not now that we've both broken all of our legs and the mill's closed down, leaving Dad redundant.'

I don't work in a mill by the way, but dull office work isn't very *Hollywood plot*. You remember Billy Elliot? Coal miner's son from Up North, had to take up ballet in secret? Well, in real life he was actually brought up in a lovely big house in Somerset and his parents were both ballet-loving, mid-ranking executives in a local fax machine manufacturer. Not sexy. Artistic license is used liberally in these films, y'know.

In seemingly unrelated-but-soon-to-be-connected news, CC2 was fitted with a pair of retainers at this point, top and bottom. These were fantastically expensive for some reason, though the shock of the cost was mildly offset by the hilarious speech impediment it gave her; she sounded like Gollum with an over-productive salivary gland.

'We learnt about kssJuliussssss kssssssCaesar in khhhhistory today, khsssssssssss'. About what?

'KsssssCaesar, khsssssss.' Come again? 'KsssssCaesar! Khsssss.' One more time? Etc. Never got boring. Are we terrible parents? Whatever.

Oh, and in case you don't have be-braced children of your own, the sound at the end of each sentence is the sucking back up of all the excess spit that somehow pooled in her mouth while trying to talk. Parenthood is a magical thing.

Anyway, she had to wear these for almost all of the day, just taking them out for meals and when she needed to be understood clearly. She was provided with a case to store them in, of course, though she usually just left them on the dining table at mealtimes, because putting them away was clearly too much effort. This case actually had a double function, in that it not only protected the braces when out of her mouth but made them harder for her to lose. Being very clumsy and forgetful, we bought the case in the brightest and most visible shade of pink they had, a move which would've worked perfectly had she ever bothered to use it.

You can probably see where this is going now, I've pretty much laid out the two threads nice and clearly and they're about to collide. That's right, CC2 lost her retainers. In the stable.

This, as ever, raised several questions. First and foremost, why were they not in her mouth at the time? Why did she feel the need to take them out in a stable, of all places?

This had an answer that raised more questions in itself — 'I was sharing a bag of Hula Hoops with the pony.'

Of course she was. She was sharing a bag of delicious hoop-shaped savoury snacks with a horse. While sat on the pissy floor doing her homework. By the light of her phone, as it turned out, though that was heartening in a way as it's usually lost somewhere. It was also just before dinner, but that should be a given at this stage, and we can probably just gloss over that.

Do horses eat Hula Hoops? Clearly, they can, but are they supposed to? From what I can glean, any nags of ours only eat the most expensive luxury food. Nothing as mundane as 'some grass' for our ponies, it's usually steamed hay and bags of stuff called something like 'Hi-Performance Premium ExpensoFeed'. And Hula Hoops, it seems.

It's the same with our cats... mouse head? 'Mmmm, yum yum!' Rabbit intestines? 'Delicious, thank you!' Slightly less expensive-than-usual cat biscuits? 'Don't fuck with me, human. Get your lousy hand back in your pocket or I'll shit in the bath again.'

The next question related to where she left her retainers while feasting on said salty tubular treats. In the fitted case they came with, presumably, stuffed for safety into a pocket? No. On the floor. Of course they were. On the floor, with the piss.

This lead to CC1 spending a couple of hours sifting through the entire contents of the stable by hand, like a desperate lottery winner down at the town dump after accidentally binning the life-changing ticket. She did turn up one of the retainers. Not the full pair, but just the one. This meant that either her sifting skills weren't all that, or else the nag was now likely to get its teeth straightened. I'm assuming she checked the horse for an amusing speech impediment and plumped for the first option because she then had to borrow a metal detector to scan the stable. You couldn't make this shit up, you really couldn't.

Amazingly, she managed to find the second brace with

the metal detector, and everything was back to where it ought to be — except the bastard nag which was still in our stable. The retainers were put in a glass of boiling water to be thoroughly sterilised, CC2 was placed in the doghouse, and the metal detector was given back to whoever the hell lent it to CC1. Who has a metal detector, anyway? Presumably, someone who wanted to find Roman gold rather than some manky plastic and wire, covered in wood shavings stuck on with spittle and horse piss, but them's the breaks.

I'm not entirely sure whether this particular episode will make the inspirational nags-to-riches movie of CC2's life completely intact. The endearing scene of little girl and pony spending time together doing homework might be sullied a bit by the sight of the mother subsequently sifting through the pissy bedding looking for a lost retainer.

Also, the movie would probably be spoilt by the viewer not being able to understand a word the girl says. 'Yesssch, kkdresshage practish later, ksssssssss.'

No. Better with the artistic license, I think. Lose the braces, keep the mill closing.

One other problem with letting a horse onto your property is that you've effectively let the genie out of the bottle. Once a precedent has been set, it stays set, and genies are famously difficult to push back in. They're quite wispy, you see, hard to get a solid purchase on.

To illustrate this point, please read the following conversation I had with CC1 whilst the nag was *chez nous*...

Me: I can't believe you put that bastard nag in the garden.

CC1: Yeah. Sorry about that. Um, there's something else I should probably tell you too...

Me: What?

CC1: Actually, it doesn't matter.

Me: Oh yes it does. What? What is it?

CC1: No, it's nothing really.

Me: Tell me...

CC1: I'll tell you later.

Me: Tell me now. It's bad, isn't it? What's it done?

CC1: No, nothing. It's done nothing. And no, it's not bad.

Me: So tell me then.

CC1: I'll tell you later.

Me: Tell me now.

CC1: I'll email you.

Me: You'll email me??

CC1: Yes, when I've left the house. I'm off out soon.

Me: You need to be out of the house to tell me? WHAT THE FUCK IS IT?!

CC1: It's nothing, honestly. It's fine.

Me: It's so fine that you need to be out of the house to tell me? What is it? Tell me!

CC1: I'll tell you later. I'm going out now, I'm taking the pony and CC2 to a lesson.

She left me goggle-eyed, brain fizzing with awful mental images of the nag having dug a massive hole to try and burrow out, or eaten a neighbour's cat.

An hour or two later though, and I'd forgotten the whole thing and went outside to think about mowing the lawn. In the stiffening breeze, I could hear the sounds of the countryside. Wind mainly, but also a distant dog barking and a horse whinnying nearby. Ah, the nag's making a bit of a racket, I thought, probably spooked by the sun or a cloud. But then I remembered that they'd just left with the pony and I'd actually watched them drive off with it. Must be one of the neighbour's horses then, I thought.

Wait... *neighbour's* horses? What are we, Amish? Our neighbours are decent, normal people. They have cats, maybe a dog. No horses. So what the fuck just whinnied?

I turned my head slowly to the left and nearly shat myself. There was a bastard horse in my garden, but not even our bastard horse. Some other bastard's bastard horse! And not even a full-size horse either, but one of those stupid Shitlands. At this point, I realised the significance of one of CC1's friends being over the previous day — the one that owns Shitlands. The little cow (CC1 I mean, not the friend... though, y'know), had conspired to bring other people's spare horses into my garden now, on top of our own, which was absolutely bad enough to start with.

Well, now I knew 'the secret', so I texted CC1 angrily; 'What the fuck is that in the garden? I've seen it. Some living Breyer horse wandering around.'

No reply.

Later that day, the CCs came home, and I was waiting for them.

Me: Did you get my texts earlier?
CC1: No. (She lied)
Me: Well, I know your secret. I saw it!
CC1: Ah, I see.

Me: Yes, indeed. And I know whose it is too. I worked it out. Why is he in our garden?
CC1: He? No, they're both mares.

Long pause

Me, very slowly: What... do... you... mean... "They"?

Longer pause

CC1: Turns out you didn't know the secret after all, I guess!
Me: What do you mean? Are you telling me there are two fucking Breyers in the garden??

CC1 was now laughing uncontrollably

Me: This isn't funny! Why is the first one there, anyway?
CC1: To keep the pony company.
Me: SO WHAT'S THE SECOND ONE DOING THERE?
CC1: To keep the first one company.

Yes, the nag had staff now in the shape of two comically small 'horses' who were seconded to act as security detail and to keep wolves and bears away, but also as company. Which was ironic as it turned out because they hated each other. Like I say, once the genie is out of the bottle, then all bets are off, and the nags start multiplying like

Gremlins in water. Or is it when they're fed after midnight? Either way, one pony rapidly became three, or one and two halves at the very least.

Of course, when our own pony first turned up, I was not only promised that it would be a brief visit but that there would be actual benefits. 'Just think, you won't have to mow the grass in the paddock,' I was told in an encouraging tone, 'and it'll look idyllic with a beautiful pony standing around looking serene'. My biggest fear was that the ground would be damaged and that my years of slowly turning the rough old paddock from a mess of nettles into a smart garden would be wasted. CC1 assured that me that, being summer, the ground was hard and dry and that the grass would be lovingly nibbled into perfect neatness.

This turned out to be complete bollocks, of course, as we live in England and therefore 'summer' is merely the season with the least-cold rain. Her promises turned out to be completely baseless, much like the wet turf, and the nag left the place looking like the surface of a giant golf ball. As it turns out, horses do sometimes stand around looking serene, but also spend a certain amount of time sprinting wildly around in tight circles, carving up the ground like it's made of soft cheese. Where a single horse is capable of making a decent mess, three playing together is total chaos.

In the meantime, the CCs made plans on where the next nag hotel was to be. I had assumed, naively as it transpired, that the new place had already been booked and that the reason the pony had to come and stay was merely that there was a day or two in between the two bookings. In reality, they had no plans at all and spent several weeks slowly visiting every hotel in about a 50-mile radius to inspect them. I didn't accompany them on any of these trips, of course; I'd rather stick my privates in the microwave, but I can visualise exactly what the process would've been. I see them like proper hotel inspectors, with clipboards, hardhats and hi-vis jackets, running fingers along tack room shelves to check for dust and scribbling little notes while making furtive, sidelong glances at each other.

Of course, as it was for the precious nag, they took it even more seriously than actual hotel inspectors would for mere humans. I'm pretty sure they took soil samples and measured air quality as well as surveying all the existing customers at length. The pony can only be hosed down with water between 19.3 and 19.8 degrees, y'know, these things can't just be left to chance.

Eventually, after the knock-out rounds had whittled down the selection to the best of the best, the finalists were invited to submit their proposals, and after a series of gruelling interviews like at the end of *The Apprentice*, a new nag hotel was crowned the winner.

This was excellent news and meant that all the horses we'd accrued could now leave and that my garden was once again 100% horse-free, which, like a *Tesco's Value* burger, is exactly as they're supposed to be in theory.

There was one small issue, of course. Have you ever seen those photos from Glastonbury the day after it ends, with acres of rubbish and abandoned tents and stuff everywhere? Well, it was a bit like that. The first thing I noticed was the enormous pile of gently steaming shit that was stacked up on one side of the garden. Even Glastonbury doesn't sink that low. And so, I had to start mowing a little path around the manure mountain, which just emphasised it even more, if anything, like I was tending to a monument of some kind as the groundskeeper.

CC1 informed me that this was to go on to flower beds come the spring, but as our 'flower' beds are usually 3-foot deep in weeds, I wasn't confident that would really help anything, apart from the weeds. And no matter how 'natural' and 'rich in nutrients' horse manure is, according to CC1's repeated protestations, it was just a big pile of shit at the end of the day.

Then there was everything else — empty plastic sacks blowing across the garden like modern-day tumbleweeds, shovels and forks, wheelbarrows and bags of rubbish. Plus a light covering of hay absolutely everywhere, like an equine version of snow. And was my garage cleared out of all the nag junk that was being stored there while the horse stayed over? I'll give you two guesses. There were boxes of horse stuff with horse things leaning against them, and other assorted horse items everywhere. I didn't know what half the things were and didn't much wish to know. I just knew that I didn't like them, in all their annoying pinkness.

After clearing up the garden, I then had to tackle the stable itself. CC2 is a lovely little worker when she's at the hotel; I've watched her diligently clean and scrub everything after use, it's a beautiful thing to watch. Beautiful mainly because I never get to see anything of the sort at home. Clean and polish the rigging? No problem. Sweep the stable? Twice a day. Make sure everything is put back into the tacky room exactly as it was found? Of course. Tidy your bedroom? No fucking chance.

Sadly, our own stable fell into the category of 'home' rather than 'a proper horse hotel' so all cleaning and maintenance was left to me. It's a blue job, apparently. So, armed with power tools, rubble bags and any other equipment I could lay my hands on, I went in to tackle it. And what a sight it was.

Firstly, there was hay. Piles of it. Mountains of it. I burnt a significant amount, but there was still tonnes left. And the stuff that was hiding under it! Once I'd cleared it all out, I found a family of rats, £2.31 in change, some half-finished homework, half a bag of Hula Hoops, a mug, three forks, more hay, an old lawnmower I didn't know we even had, the remains of Lord Lucan and two Japanese soldiers who didn't know the war had ended. They weren't even aware of each other, they'd been living in different piles.

And what's with the buckets? Why are there always so many buckets everywhere? I cleared out 143 wobbly buckets that couldn't even maintain their own shape properly, in every colour of the rainbow from pink to a pinky-purple. Some were brand new, some worn, some empty, some full to the brim with horse shit. How many buckets does one horse need? How many can a person hold at any one time?

I then drove to the tip 14 times, dumping endless small sections of rope, mouldy tubs of salty gunk, and empty sacks of various nag food. I can't tell you how tiring it was.

But, the good news was that the stable was eventually devoid of all signs that there were once horses in it, just as stables ought to be. The chickens were happy, I was happy (if knackered and unable to bend more than 14 degrees at the waist) and we now had a lovely, clean space at the end of the garden. Finally, I had the place back to build that sex dungeon.

And so, eventually, that particular chapter came to a close. It was supposed to be very brief when it started, like a chapter in a short story, or even a page in a pamphlet. But it ended up like a chapter in a Dostoevsky novel: much longer than I'd hoped, full of misery and poverty and ultimately, pretty hard going. And all in a completely foreign language that I didn't understand.

So please listen carefully, and mark my words, for your own good: Never. Let. A. Horse. Onto. Your. Property.

The thing about a horse is
It's not a human being
There's just no point in trying to teach it chess or water-skiing

It needs a house to live in
With straw and hay and salt licks
It doesn't need a sofa or TV with built-in Netflix

You might think you want closeness
But no, I beg your pardon
You'd be amazed to see the mess it would make of your garden

So when you choose a stable
Take care of the location
And try to find one miles away whatever the temptation

CHAPTER 5

Don't think it isn't about the horse

DON'T THINK IT ISN'T ABOUT THE HORSE

I f you were to track down a nag-free person (just look for someone clean and freely spending disposable money) and ask them how any future horse ownership would affect them, they'd most likely give you some pretty standard and obvious answers, depending on whether they thought it was a good thing or not. If they were to concentrate on the positives, then they might wax lyrical about all the wonderful, early morning hacks into the countryside they'd have, the finding of a new, four-legged best friend, or all the rosettes they'd win at competitions. A less horse-inclined person might concentrate more on the cons than the pros — the nagatives, if you will — and reel off the usual list of complaints about expense, shovelling shit and spending too much time driving back and forth to nag hotels.

The reality of the situation is that there's a little of both, and very few people get to live a whole horse life experiencing just the items from one of those lists. Even the most ardent horse person will complain a little when they get dragged face-first into three feet of wet mud while their wellies are left several feet behind them, and even the least horsey person will occasionally see the beauty in young ponies frolicking in a summer meadow at sunset.

My experience of the last decade, however, suggests that the impact horses will have on your life isn't just the mixture of fairly obvious things listed above, but much more than that. Horses have a way of creeping into little areas of your life in ways you would never have predicted beforehand, and even ignoring the obvious things like the house and bank balance, a wide range of items and possessions end up getting 'horsed'.

Now, a lot of horse people have lorries to chauffeur their nags around in, and this seems logical enough. Horses tend to be quite big and you generally can't get them into the back of a car even if you fold the seats down, but when you think about it, horses have played a blinder here. If you go back a century and look at any old photos of cities, towns or anywhere else with roads, you'll notice something straight away. There'll be horses everywhere towing a wide range of contraptions behind them to move people around in. People domesticated the horse so that, among other things, they could travel around with greater efficiency and comfort, essentially letting the horse do all the work. Fast forward to today, and wherever you look in the countryside, you see horses being driven around by people, often in hugely expensive lorries with every luxury in the back to ensure the horse is as comfortable as possible.

I don't know whether all the horses got together to hatch a plan or not, but somehow they really managed to beat us at our own game, and you have to hand it to them. That said, it's not entirely necessary for every horse owner to have a lorry as they don't all need to travel great distances very often. Much like the horses themselves, lorries and smaller, cheaper trailers can be rented so that they're only paid for when needed.

There's been a recurring conversation in our house over the years that goes something like this:

CC1: Will you buy us a lorry?
Me: Nope.

To me, it seems a bit ridiculous that we need our own whole lorry. Normal people don't own lorries; that's a specialist interest for people with names like Big Dave or Eddie Stobart. I've resisted the regular requests over the years to spend many thousands of pounds I don't have on something that would only get used a few times each year and insisted that CC1 just hires a trailer whenever necessary.

This makes me happy in theory but does mean that her car gets pressed into horse-related action a little more than it would otherwise, and is used not just for towing but for the ferrying around of hay and straw and the storage of all kinds of nag-related crap. The thing is piled high inside with boots and whips and salt licks and a thousand items, recognisable or otherwise. It has been well and truly horsed and I'm not sure it's recoverable.

I'd add a photo of the inside, but you'd just talk about us and then report us to the council's sanitation department, or whatever they have. Either way, men in hazmat suits would turn up and erect a big white tent around the car, maybe the whole house. It'd be like the ending bit in E.T. with loads of polythene tunnels and bleeping machines. Maybe Greenpeace would get involved and start some kind of cleanup operation, once all the scientific experiments had been allowed to take place.

If I was prepared to spend an hour or two emptying the car, I'd be not in the least bit surprised to find a bedraggled seagull covered in oil, to be honest. Probably being looked after by some uncontacted pygmy tribe who'd been living in the saddle holders under the pile of coats and jodhpurs, only venturing out at night to hunt for wild Haribo.

That all pales into insignificance, though, when I tell you that I actually found some grass growing on it recently. I'm serious. The back bumper was home to so much partly composted hay and straw that several blades of fresh grass and something else that possibly resembled clover had taken root and started to flourish. Where will this end if left unchecked? Will the whole car eventually become turf? Maybe we could make use of it as a kind of mobile picnic venue which we could drive to somewhere nice and then eat sandwiches on the roof.

'I must take the car to get cleaned,' is a phrase often heard around these parts, usually followed a few hours later by 'I didn't get chance to get the car cleaned.' I might just do it myself next weekend before any trees start growing out of the engine bay, obscuring the view forward. I don't recall reading this anywhere, but it's bound to be an MOT failure, an advisory at the very least. I can see the next report now:

Reason(s) for failure:
- Front N/S brake pads worn below limit
- Excessive rust on rear suspension mounts
- Young oak sapling in driver's line of vision

Monitor and repair if necessary (advisories):
• Rear tailgate opening impeded by wild meadow

In all seriousness, I should probably get it cleaned before its next MOT. I'd hate for them to find a breeding pair of great nested newts or some rare bat we hadn't noticed hanging from the roof lining. It'd get designated a conservation area and taken off the road, and then how will the nags get fed?

You could argue that it's predictable CC1's car gets horsed (and possibly that it's my own fault as I won't buy a lorry) but my own possessions should really be safer. Not so.

I bought myself a present a while back, something just for me. I smashed the piggy bank, reached down the back of the sofa, emptied my pockets, and sold some old shit on eBay. I then swept all the coins together across the kitchen table with the crook of my arm, counted it up and then spent it as quickly as possible, before anyone could so much as say 'Ooh, LeMieux have a new autumn collection out'. And I bought a drone.

It doesn't match with anything's numbnuts, it doesn't need stabling and it most certainly doesn't smell of horse shit or have hay all over it. It's dark matt grey, it's got four motors, it records video in 4k, it can go 45mph, and it's mine, all mine.

So, what was the first thing I did with it, given the endless number of creative possibilities? I could've recorded sweeping vistas, lakes and woodlands in stunning detail, or put it into 'chase' mode to follow friends in cars or motorbikes on twisty roads.

Or, I could've got dragged down to the horse hotel to video CC2 having a dressage lesson from a bird's-eye view.

Yes, of course, why didn't I think of that? What a perfect way to put the latest feat of technological engineering to use.

So the poor drone, who'd been looking forward to being sent on all kinds of adrenaline-fuelled aerial missions involving speed, danger and excitement, instead spent its first morning hanging sullenly in the sky, completely stationery at an unexciting 175 feet while pointing its little camera straight down into 1200 square metres of sand and grey stuff with a small girl on a pony walking around in it a bit. I actually felt sorry for my mechanical friend, the poor bastard.

If you were to study the footage carefully, you'd be able to see that matchy matchy was being fully employed, as usual. It was *Never Never Navy* that day, I believe. You can't really make out that the trainer had her head at 45 degrees, but trust me, the angle of dangle was all present and correct.

What you can't quite see is me, just out of shot, sat bored on the grass, holding a funky, hi-tech remote control and doing nothing with it at all. I wanted to go out again later and do something more exciting with it, but CC1 made me show her all the footage first, in slow motion, so she could check on the straightness of all the lines and the accuracy of all the circles.

It seems that anything I buy gets dragged unwillingly into some kind of equine duty, there's always a horse-related angle to everything that I didn't quite see coming. If I buy a new camera, it has to be used to photograph CC2 and the nag, if I buy a new lawnmower then I have to mow a miniature dressage arena into the garden, and if I buy a new electric screwdriver, then the first thing I have to do is head down to the hotel to fit some rug holder to a wall. This is why I spend as much as I can on wine — none of the others in the house like it, although in fairness I'm not sure if the pony's actually tried it.

CC2 commandeered my electric screwdriver for herself recently, not for anything as sensible as installing a rug holder, but still to do something horse-related, naturally. Now, CC2 is a lovely girl in many ways and has a range of talents: she can make a pony walk in circles, of course, and she's quite handy at netball, plus she can bake a decent batch of chocolate brownies. Physical coordination, however, is not something she was endowed with in any great quantities, and nor is being tidy. Combine those two things together and it's no wonder that I regularly threaten to buy her a bib and sippy cup for dinner times. Getting a forkful of food from her plate to her mouth without somehow ejecting it into the air or knocking a glass over is something she can only manage about 60% of the time, and so when I found my toolbox open, alarm bells started to ring.

With eyes narrowed in suspicion, I walked slowly to the kitchen, rather concerned at the mess I'd find there, but the sight that met me was actually worse than I'd even imagined. There was a mess, of course, sure. A horrible mess, in fact, with bits of fruit and vegetable all over the place, lumps, skin and juice all over the work surface and quite a lot of the floor, too. It looked very much like a small bomb had gone off in a greengrocery. What was more alarming, though, was CC2 herself, standing in the middle of it all, pale-faced, holding an impressively bloodied tissue around her finger and crying. She told me at this point that she was feeling very faint, but although I now spotted several more bloodied tissues lying amongst the bits of vegetables, it wasn't the loss of blood that was making her light-headed, but merely the sight of it, which she'd just discovered she had a serious aversion to.

Eventually, she calmed down, the blood stopped flowing, and I hunted around for a plaster while humming the theme tune to Casualty, and once she was mended, she finished the task in hand, which turned out to be the inventive creation of a snack treat for the nag. What she was trying to do was to thread various chunks of fruit and veg onto a length of string which could then be hung in the pony's hotel room for him to nibble on at his leisure. A sort of nag kebab, if you will.

The instructions for creating this snackdangler appeared to be as follows, from what I later managed to ascertain:

Step 1

Sweep the kitchen for every piece of fruit and vegetable you can find that a horse might potentially be interested in. CC2 selected apples, carrots, swede and parsnips. I'm not 100% sure what swede is, or why we had any in the first place, (and, spoiler alert, apparently the nag wasn't that arsed either), so I'd treat these as optional.

Step 2

Search the kitchen for some kind of string, twine, etc. She eventually found some in the drawer full of old shit, under a Chinese takeaway menu from 2012 and some cocktail sticks that had fallen out of their plastic box and nobody had ever been bothered to put back.

Step 3
Raid the toolbox for something sharp and dangerous. Anything really, as long as it's not actually designed for making holes in things. An electric screwdriver perhaps. There's no way on earth that this could go wrong in any way.

Step 4
Utilising said inappropriate tool, try to force holes in your assorted fruit and veg. Make as much mess as you absolutely can, this is vital. There should be bits of apple peel and chunks of veg all over the shop if you can manage it, and bonus points for juice stains on the ceiling.

Step 5
Thread the mangled food lumps onto the string.

Step 6
Pick the food lumps up from the floor.

Step 7
Remember to tie a knot at the end of the string before adding the food lumps next time.

Step 8
Repeat Step 5

Then, take the finished nibblestring down to the nag hotel, hang it up and watch as the horse attempts to eat from it. Depending on the greed and intelligence levels of your particular sportscow, this may lead to all the grub being eaten quickly, repeated failed attempts to get any purchase on it whatsoever or complete disinterest. CC2 got mainly (b) from the pony, though (c) if you're just talking about the swede.

The above list does miss out one important step which CC2 managed to include after Step 4, so I'll just add that one now.

Step 4.5
After trying and failing to make suitable holes with the electric screwdriver, grab a steak knife from the cutlery drawer. Then, pushing down as hard as you can onto a shiny, round apple, try to slip, cutting your finger as deeply as you can manage. Start crying.

I suggested that next time she tries making a nag kebab, she should probably wear her riding hat and some protective clothing in case she cuts herself and actually does faint and keel over. One of those airbag jackets would be best I suppose, with the cord attached to the work surface, but I'm not forking out for one of those just for fruit cutting, so I suggested maybe just spreading a few cushions on the floor behind her. She didn't find it very funny, though.

I'm afraid that once a horse has been allowed to enter your life, very little of it will remain untouched in some way. It's very easy to make the mistake of confusing horse riding with other hobbies that can be picked up and put away again neatly like, oh I dunno, playing the harmonica. Harmonicas have very little in common with horses, except perhaps that they can make quite unpleasant noises if things are going badly, and they can have quite a lot of slobber on them. But that's pretty much it. What harmonicas don't tend to do is try to take over other aspects of your life and are generally very undemanding of your time and resources, outside of the bits of your week when you fancy actually playing the thing.

The other enormous benefit of harmonicas is that they are cheap, don't require their own houses, their own transport, saddles, insurance, and... oh my God... WHY DIDN'T I JUST BUY CC2 A HARMONICA ALL THOSE YEARS AGO?

Sorry about that, I think I've calmed down now. But I'm definitely about to go and browse harmonicas online, they sound great! They also don't take up too much room in the way that horses do, as the next chapter will hopefully illustrate.

Now you might think that life's a blend
Of things to do and time to spend

So many ways to fill your day
It could be work, it could be play

And though you see variety
Alone and in society

I've just one point to reinforce
That everything's about the horse

CHAPTER 6

Defend your territory

DEFEND YOUR TERRITORY

Fancy playing a game of word association? You do? Excellent, me too! OK, without further ado, let's play...

Fish.

I say 'chips'. I win.

I think already we're starting to see some of the problems of playing this game in a book. Firstly, I can't hear you so I'm not really able to consider your answers, and secondly it's likely that I wrote this ages ago now, so I've probably moved on with my life and am currently doing something else entirely, like shopping in a supermarket or sleeping. Still, that's life I'm afraid, one-nil to me. What's that? You think it's unfair? Minus one point to you for arguing with the ref. I'm now 2-0 up. Ha!

Oh yes, the third thing about this game is that I control the scoring.

OK, let's continue...

Horse.

I say 'expense'. I don't care what you say, it could be 'love', 'freedom', 'riding', 'harmony' or whatever other airy-fairy whale music bollocks you come up with, but we all know my answer's right. 3-0.

OK, here's the big one...

House.

I say 'people'. Seems obvious enough, doesn't it? A house is a building for people to live in that stops rain from falling on them. And inside it, there's room to store all the people stuff that we have — clothes, food, wine, PlayStations, that kind of thing.

Horses have their own kind of houses as well, in the form of nag hotels. There they have rooms for living in, and also a separate area for storing all their crap that's called the 'tacky room', and this is where you'll find all the rigging and the naghats and the matchy matchy shit and so on.

So far, so good. It's a solid, workable system and shouldn't be that hard to understand. In theory at least, the people and the horses live in their own separate buildings, along with all their possessions. But as is so often the case, the difference between theory and practice is negligible in theory but quite large in practice. What I've noticed happen is what I like to term 'encroachment': the slow and gradual process whereby horse stuff seems to start appearing in my human house. At first, it's just a single item, like a hat maybe, that appears on the dining table one day with a promise that it'll be gone soon, but instead it gets company in the form of a whip. If it ended there, then it wouldn't be so bad, but it doesn't end there, does it? No, it does not.

Here's a gardening tip for you, by the way... never, under any circumstances, plant bamboo in your garden. It's pure evil. Or more specifically, certain types of bamboo are. My understanding from reading up on the subject is that bamboo is either the kind that grows in clumps or the kind that grows underground in different directions and pops up all over the place where you least expect it. We have that one. Little bits of bamboo sprout up about 30 feet from the actual plant itself and have to be attacked like a Whac-A-Mole as soon as you see them. Also, the stuff grows so incredibly fast that you wouldn't believe it. I chop it down every now and again, but as soon as I turn my back, it pops back up, and when I swing around to check my work, it's ten feet tall again. You can pretty much see it growing, and if you hold your ear close to the thing, you can hear a little squeaking noise as it stretches and grows in front of your eyes. Like I say, it's evil. I've tried browsing on the Dark Web to see if I could buy a panda to stick in there, but I've had no such luck so far and have now resigned myself to the fact that the bamboo has won and will stay there forever.

Horse stuff is basically the bamboo of our house and if left unchecked, it'll spread its little tendrils into every room and space until you can't move for numbnuts and salt licks.

What you need to do is to fight: to stand your ground

and try to repel the attack that will come from all sides. It's an uphill battle, I'm afraid, but you can't just let them win and let your own house become an extension of the nag hotel. It's bad enough having nags in the nag hotel in the first place, but it's another thing entirely when they start moving all their shit into your own home.

In terms of the ongoing war for control of my house, I can't now recall with certainty which territory fell into enemy hands first, but I think it was the utility room. There were several skirmishes leaving casualties of numbnuts and leg warmers, but sadly that's a battle I ultimately lost, and enemy forces have been occupying that room since then. You can't move in there for matchy matchy shit, stirrups, tubs of salt (why?) and all the other usual horse crap, and occasionally it's even used as some kind of supply depot with large sacks of horse food filling up the place. You can't always open the door to get in these days and have to abseil down from the bedroom and in through the window.

The chest freezer is the main storage table and appears to be very useful for rolling up newly washed legwarmers on, and then leaving them there to be stored indefinitely, sometimes stashed away in little plastic cases, or sometimes just left there in piles. I've no idea what's actually in the freezer anymore as I can't open the thing, but I assume it's frozen horse treats.

The washing machine can be used for 'clothes' apparently, but you have to jump in there pretty quickly if you see it empty. Usually, it's a spinning kaleidoscope of Visa Violet and Babysick Beige.

The kitchen, too, is most definitely a lost cause and is probably the command centre of the whole pony operation. I think it's just because people tend to hang out in kitchens, like at parties, but it gets used for a whole range of naguine activities. Naturally, there's usually a clothes dryer in there, full of matchy matchy shit that's just come out of the washing machine, but it's also the main storage zone for nag mags, formal prancing score sheets and those things we laminate that explain which direction to go in at X — 'trot maps' I think they're called. They litter every available surface.

The kitchen also acts as a kind of holding area for rosettes before they eventually wend their way up to CC2's bedroom around 6-8 months after arriving.

It's not just for storage though, oh no siree. No, it's far more sinister than that. I came home from work recently to find the oven cooling, and the kitchen filled with baking smells — generally a good sign. On opening the fridge, my hopes were confirmed, and I saw a plate of little cupcakes looking all chocolatey and delicious. Marvellous, I thought, and only a Tuesday too!

I reached in to grab one and was halfway towards shoving it into my gob when I noticed something was awry. On closer inspection, it didn't actually look chocolatey, but more like something the dog deposits after it's been eating leaves. 'What the fuck is this?' I said out loud, before carefully placing it back in the fridge, and washing my hands thoroughly.

Yes, you've guessed it, CC2 was baking for the pony and filling the fridge with its 'treats'. Next to these was a bag of carrots which were apparently for the nag too. It basically has its own section of the fridge. And the fruit bowl — 'Don't take the green apples, they're for the pony', CC2 told me as I was getting my lunch the next day. Yep, the kitchen has definitely fallen into enemy hands.

I wouldn't be surprised if I came down to breakfast

and found the nag sat at the kitchen table, reading the paper while wearing my dressing gown. I can picture it now: as I open the fridge, a pair of bifocals peer over the top of the paper and say 'I've used up the last of the milk I'm afraid. Terribly sorry.'

For some reason, I imagine its voice is like David Niven or something — posh and polite on the face of it, but with an air of uncaring, sneering arrogance under the surface. 'Why don't you have toast instead?' it'd say without looking up from the paper. And as I snarl internally and march towards the bread bin, I'd hear 'I think there's still the crust left at least — I had the rest earlier. Terribly sorry.'

The dining room is an overflow zone for numbnuts that have been washed in the utility room, dried in the kitchen and now need storing somewhere until needed but can't fit in the utility room because it's already full. The cats sleep on them here. They're blissfully unaware that their bed, made from 18 layers of Stockholm Syndrome's finest, cost more than my own bed, and probably my car. They don't give a shit either, of course, cos they're cats.

It goes without saying that CC2's bedroom is probably controlled by occupying forces. I can't say for certain as I try to avoid going in there, but from what I've seen it's basically a nag shrine. The distant whinnying of wild ponies plays on a loop over the stereo, the air is filled with the scent of 'Fresh Straw and Horse Piss' candles, and a framed photo of the god Valegro is almost completely obscured now by tea lights, petals and daily offerings. The walls are a blur of red, blue, and yellow. And good luck to her, this is off my patch, she can have that one.

You'd think perhaps that it would only be the house

itself that's under attack, but you'd be very wrong. Let's talk about the garage.

So, we have a garage at our house. Not unusual. I didn't even just inherit it with the house though, I actually had it built. When we moved in, there was some ancient, run-down little hut which looked like the kind of place you'd expect to find discarded syringes and old cans of Special Brew, and the doorway was so narrow you could only fit cars made before 1970 in. So, at enormous expense, I had it knocked down and replaced with a shiny new double garage in which I could keep cars and motorbikes and tools I don't use and other man stuff. I was very excited at this prospect, and in the early days of its existence, I did just as I'd planned and kept my car in there, all dry and warm and safe. Of course, I eventually had to sell the car to afford all the nag shit, and just to rub it in, this then began to take up the space in the garage that I'd originally used for the car. Like a weed, I tell you... it started off just around the edges, little piles of buckets and brushes and things. And then brooms started appearing, and wheelbarrows, and bales of hay, and electric fence equipment and, eventually, a whole fucking horse. Admittedly, that was a one-off when CC2 decided she needed to groom the pony out of the rain one day, but I think that it illustrates the kind of contempt they have for my garage that I was once so proud of and excited about.

Anyway, I eventually decided that enough was enough, and I took affirmative action to try and restore some kind of order. I bought three big shelving units and spent a long, long time screwing them together. I even spent a whole load of extra time and money and brushed both sides of the shelves with some kind of special sealant to ensure a long and sag-free life. What can I say, I'm a details guy.

Once completed, I said to CC1 and CC2, ahem (this is me talking to them now), ahem, I said, behold the lovely new shelving units. There is much in the way of tools and car parts of various shapes and colours... sorry, I don't know why I started writing that like some weird medieval minstrel, I'll start again...

Look here, I said, I've spent hours building those bastards and I'm fucking knackered. I'm going to the pub. I want you to tidy all your horse shit up and stack it away nicely so I can actually see the garage floor again. You can have the whole of that left-hand unit and I'll come back later and put all my stuff on the other two. Deal? Ok, off you go.

Anyway, I quickly realised my mistake, of course. Left-hand unit, my arse. If you were to come and look at the shelving now, you'd be able to make out a little collection of cans of oil and stuff that are mine in a small spot at the top somewhere. And that's it. That's what they left me. On my shelves. In my garage. The space in front of the shelves is also filled with all kinds of other crap, so I can barely even get to my stuff if I needed to.

I didn't even know what most of it is. I mean, I recognise boots, because I've seen boots before, but these ones look expensive. They probably were, and I probably bought them. There's also a saddle, perched on a cat house for some reason and then a whole load of matchy matchy shit and horse stroking equipment. Also, a lot of tubs, presumably full of salt, and it goes without saying that there are hundreds of buckets too, I think these buckets must breed in the dark.

I'm technically middle-aged now and should be filling

that garage with some ridiculous little sports car or something, but I can't because I don't have any money left, and now I've got nowhere to put the bastard. Oh, I have a lovely garage, yes. But there's no room in it anymore for cars, it's just one more tack room, like the kitchen and the utility room.

The rest of the house is basically a lost cause, too. If not used for actual storage, then it's usually just covered in a light dusting of hay. I found some in our bed just this morning, and I'm not even joking. Most men that have just found some hay on her side of the marital bed would probably wonder what their wife's been up to, but I know already. Cleaning up horse shit. I'm not sure which is worse, really. I mean, I know where she's been, I suppose, but it's pretty disgusting, and not in that kind of way.

But here we come to the crux of the gist of the point of the matter. I've pretty much lost control of the house and just hide in my little study. It's like one of those maps you used to see on the news a couple of years ago — the equine ISIS control all the main territory and the good guys (me!) are holed up in some small town in the centre, taking heavy horse fire from all directions.

I'm completely besieged on all sides now, with the enemy amassing forces and seemingly able to strike at will. It's got ridiculous. What room is next? There's only our bedroom and bathroom left, and I shudder to think how those will be invaded. Is there any product available for horses that comes in tubes similar to toothpaste? I bet there is and, whatever it is, I bet it's disgusting. Probably some sort of equine haemorrhoid cream or something.

If you have horse people in your life, then be prepared to defend your territory. Stand your ground and fight to the death. I mean, you're gonna lose, just so you know, but show willing at the very least.

OK, let's continue with word association, I'll do the last one again.

House...

I say 'matchy matchy'. I lose.

I drive home in the pouring rain and park my car outside
We've got a garage just for this, but no room left; I've tried

I turn the key and try to push, but can't get through the door
There's boots and whips and tubs of salt, God only knows what for

The kitchen's full of matchy matchy waiting to be dried
They told me that they owned no blue, I see that now they lied

I try the fridge to find a snack, those cakes should do the trick
With open mouth I catch a whiff — I'm very nearly sick

There's numbnuts on the dining table, piled up four feet high
I'm sure I saw some earlier, but guess that these are dry

They don't look very stable though, stacked up so high like that
I hope it doesn't fall and scare the shit out of the cat

There used to be space everywhere, it used to be so clean
The stuff we owned was kept in drawers and very rarely seen

But that was back when all we had was kids and pets, of course
I didn't factor storing stuff owned by a bloody horse

CHAPTER 7

What's in it for me?

WHAT'S IN IT FOR ME?

There's no easy way of saying this, so I'll come straight out with it: there's basically nothing in it for you.

There, I said it. You can pretty much just skip to the next chapter now if you like, this one's gonna be pretty short.

There are plenty of downsides to having horse people in your life, and for examples of this, just read any other part of this book. And all of the last book. And anything else ever written about horses. I mean, sure, the horse people themselves presumably get some kind of sick pleasure from riding around on the nags, even if they themselves seem to moan quite a lot about the mud and the rain and the shitpicking and everything else, but none of the benefits appear to be particularly transferable. If a child or partner of yours is really into, I don't know, carpentry, for example, then you might get a free cupboard out of it, or a rabbit hutch, or whatever other wood-based product that you may require. If perhaps they're into sailing, then they'll be able to take you out for the day so you can feel the wind in your hair as you skate across the open water and find a nice harbour or lakeside pub for a spot of lunch.

But spending time with your horse people? Here, take this old bucket, fill it with shit and try not to let anything bite you. Only four more hours and then you can hose yourself down and respond to that pile of bills over there.

Ace.

Occasionally there are suggestions of great personal benefits to come, but these tend to be pretty empty promises. For example, when catching CC1 browsing online for expensive luxury horse boxes, she'll often try to turn the tables and make it sound like it could be all of our dreams come true.

'Imagine what you'd be able to do with it when we're not using it,' she said once, with great enthusiasm, 'just think of all the things you could fit inside it to take wherever you pleased!'

'Like what?'

She had to think for a moment.

'Um... I don't know... er... a horse?'

Exactly.

She's often suggested that I should get a horse myself, in a blatant attempt to get me on board with the whole thing, presumably with the end result that I fall in love with it all and sell the house and car to buy a yard and lorry. She even booked me a lesson once, behind my back, and announced it to me like it was some kind of shit birthday present. I didn't like it. If you can picture a scowling middle-aged man sat on a bored horse, walking in circles at a snail's pace and both wishing it would end, then that would be about right. Let's just say that it didn't rub off on me, and when the next lesson was due, I fled the country and lived under an assumed name for a year in South America, doing menial work as a labourer to save up for reconstructive surgery to get a new face so that I could return safely.

No, there's not much in it for you, I'm afraid. If you have young children that are desperate for a hobby to fill their lives and they've got a birthday coming up, then I definitely don't suggest buying an introductory riding lesson, whatever you do. How about a nice wood saw, or perhaps a chisel? It'll be the gift that keeps on giving, trust me.

In some ways I
Just blame myself
For that sixth birthday present
A pony riding lesson then
Had seemed so very pleasant

It's not that I
Begrudge the cash
It costs to fuel her passion
But not all children spend it like
It's going out of fashion

I've bought a horse
I've bought it clothes
I've nearly bought a lorry
I seemed to have bought something now
In every category

I sometime think
That birthday gift
Could maybe have been better
If I'd just bought a knitting set
I'd have a lovely sweater

CHAPTER 8

Never buy a horse

NEVER BUY A HORSE

We live in a consumer society, so they say, and buy things in ever-increasing amounts, whether we need them or not. It's never been easier either, and long-gone are the days when you had to do anything as tedious as wait for the shops to open so you could trudge around for hours looking for the thing you wanted. No, these days all you have to do is tap your phone a few times in the right places and within about seven minutes some guy in a tatty van will pull up and get you to sign for your Amazon delivery.

Yesterday, some guy turned up out of the blue and handed me a parcel I didn't even remember ordering. I took it inside and when I switched on the light to see what it was, the bulb blew. Inside the box was a new lightbulb; the guy had literally come from the future to deliver the thing I hadn't even realised I needed yet. Amazing.

Sometimes we buy things that we genuinely need and can't do without, like food or shampoo. Other times it's something we need in principle, but we splash out more than is strictly necessary, like on a new car or an overly expensive watch. Sometimes it's something completely frivolous and impossible to justify, but that you see for sale and can't resist. Like, I don't know, a 1920s wind-up gramophone. What idiot owns a 1920s wind-up gramophone? you might well think. Well, um, I do. It was so obviously irresistible to me that it was actually CC1 who spotted it and knew I'd be physically unable not to buy it. We'd just whiled away a pleasant Sunday morning traipsing around an enormous antiques market when she suddenly stopped, rolled her eyes and pointed, knowing full well that we were about to spend the next ten minutes tidying the boot of the car to make room for it. It's completely impractical, of course, and you have to get up every four minutes to turn the record over, replace the needle with a new one and wind it up, but it's surprisingly useful in a power cut.

Whenever you splash out and buy something expensive, it's a common thing to let your friends try it out, partly out of generosity, partly pride, and partly as an attempt to justify spending all that money in the first place. The hope is that they'll like it as much as you do, and you'll feel all warm and fuzzy inside and tell yourself that it was definitely worth spending that wad of cash on.

'This is amazing!' they'll hopefully gush with excitement, 'I'll have to get one myself!' Because if you find something you really like in life, there's just no substitute for owning one yourself.

So it might seem pretty normal for a horse person to own a horse, right? I mean, if nags are their passion and they plan on using it regularly, then it makes sense to buy one just for themselves, doesn't it?

Not so fast!

There's a famous quote from the (immensely rich, by

the way, albeit a bit dead) magazine publisher Felix Dennis who gave a specific pearl of wisdom in his guidebook to making a fortune: "If it flies, floats or fornicates, always rent it. It's cheaper in the long run." Now, ignoring the crudity of his third example, his point was a good one — even if you're stinking rich, you should ignore the temptation of owning everything just because you can afford to buy it. It's often far wiser to rent the thing and leave someone else with the purchase cost and depreciation.

He was specifically talking about planes and boats, of course, two famously expensive items to buy and run, but even they aren't as bad as horses in some ways. A horse is a living thing, you see, and quite a delicate one at that. You don't have to crash one into the ground at 200mph or steer one into rocks to break it, they often just break by themselves. And let's face it, if you looked after a plane, a boat and a horse equally well with no-expense-spared love and care, then the first two might well be as good as new after 40 years, but the horse... not so much. There's unavoidable biology at work here, I'm afraid, and your initial investment will eventually be worth nothing at some point in the future.

If we must have access to a nag, then so be it, even if I'm not happy about it. But let's just borrow someone else's, eh? It seems so much more sensible. I'm assuming Felix Dennis just wasn't into horses himself, or else he'd have mentioned them in his quote, so I feel we can amend it for him, while making it a little more tasteful at the same time. So I like to think that "If it flies, floats or foals, always rent it. It's cheaper in the long run."

This all ties in nicely with my personal philosophy of horse ownership, in which I've always insisted that we just rent nags from somebody else, essentially for these three very good reasons:

1. They're very expensive to buy
2. They're prone to breaking down
3. They're very expensive to buy

Obviously, they're pretty damned expensive to rent too, but I'd just rather keep them at arm's length and let someone else deal with actually owning the thing.

Frankly, I'd rather not have one at all, of course — my personal view on how many horses someone needs is 'zero'. It's literally a nice, round number. If you need both transport and something to stroke, then get a car and a dog like a normal person. CC2 doesn't agree with me on this, it'll be no surprise to you to learn. She told me that in an ideal world she'd like to own nine nags: a dressage pony, a 'project' dressage pony, a showjumper, a second showjumper (in the case the first gets injured), dressage and showjumper stallions (more pizzazz apparently), dressage and showjumper foals (for training and cuddling), and Valegro. She has very modest requirements, does CC2.

My response, of course, was to listen intently and nod earnestly before replying with some watered-down equivalent of 'Ha! Fat fucking chance! Good luck with marrying someone rich!' I'm a supportive parent as I'm sure you've gathered by now, though at least I've caved enough to lease horses that she can treat as her own.

A friend of mine has a daughter who really wanted a horse, so he bought her a cockatoo. This is the kind of parenting logic I can respect, though I don't think she was particularly happy with the outcome. I think she noticed. Perhaps in years to come she'll be in therapy, forever bitter that she was denied the childhood pony of her dreams, and I suspect this is a risk he was prepared to take. But whenever I tell him about the latest expenditures I have to endure for saddles, lessons, insurance and everything else, he has the last laugh as he tells me what it costs to buy the bird food: it's literally peanuts.

I have heard the theory put forward before that if you're concerned about the cost of buying your own horse, then the best thing to do is to get a little baby one, on the basis that the initial purchase price is lower and they don't cost much to raise. In my experience though, this is utter bollocks. The first thing it's important to understand here is the concept of time. Einstein's Theory of Relativity taught us that spacetime is curved, time can dilate, and time travel might even be possible by punching a shortcut through the very fabric of the universe, but most of that rarely comes into play when buying a horse. I'm afraid to say that, for practical purposes, time is linear, so unless you own a time machine, have discovered a horse-sized wormhole, or have recently taken a lot of drugs, the future will probably happen after the present. And therefore, the earlier you buy a nag, the more it costs.

Buying a horse 'now' rather than 'later' can only save you money if the horse provides some sort of income that's greater than its outgoings, so unless you find a particularly industrious nag that either works full-time as a banker or shits gold, it seems unlikely that it'll bring in more than it costs to run. Baby horses generally can't work as bankers as they're too young to have the qualifications, so you'll be relying on it shitting gold. Unfortunately, nags only shit bills. And shit.

Also, if you think that baby horses cost less to run than adult horses then you clearly don't have children. From birth to adulthood is essentially one long meal, with pauses only taken to grow out of clothes and break things. Imagine if little human children were seven feet tall and weighed a quarter of a ton? Does that sound cheap?

No, I'm afraid there's no good time to buy a nag; young or old, it makes no difference to your impending bankruptcy. It's an entirely binary decision and there are no shades of grey to it, however young or small it might be, relatively speaking. It's not like a horse is in any way subtle or occasional; you can't keep one out of sight in a drawer somewhere, or at the back of a cupboard for special occasions like, for example, an unusual hat. No... if you have a horse, you really have a horse. It's big, it's alive, and it needs feeding.

So, although I'd rather we didn't need horses at all, it appears that CC2 needs to ride one, and we seem to have had a variety of them now over the last ten years, but at least they've all been rented. I mean, seriously, what idiot would buy a horse?

On a related note, I recently bought a horse.

CC1 made me do it, of course. Well, both of them did, really, they ganged up on me. They found one they liked, presumably on the equine equivalent of Autotrader, pointed to it on the screen like the Andy character in Little Britain saying 'Want that one!' and made arrangements to go and look at it. And then they told me.

Initially, I wasn't invited along to view the nag they found on the basis that I'd probably die of boredom, which was a fair point, but I insisted on coming along out of principle. Where my credit card goes, I follow. It's a rule of mine.

Just to make it interesting and even more expensive, the one they found wasn't even in the same country as us.

Oh no, where would the fun be in that? No, it was abroad and therefore required flights and hotels, and even a day off work as the viewing was arranged during the week, for reasons I wasn't privy to.

And so, the three of us took a little holiday. It wasn't really my kind of holiday if I'm being honest. I didn't see a beach or even an interesting new city; I didn't get to dip into a pool at any point and saw not a single thing of interest to take a photo of. I didn't have any memorable meals, I didn't get drunk, I didn't chill out, I didn't even go out. No. And yet it managed to be by far and away the most expensive holiday I've ever had.

But what a souvenir I bought! I should've got a t-shirt printed up for CC2 saying 'My parents went to Europe on holiday and all I got was A FUCKING HORSE.'

I went on a trip to India once, picked up a bug and got the squits. I thought I had it quite bad, but I didn't realise how lucky I was at the time. I mean, sure, I felt sick, had to pay a few quid at the chemist's, and I even shat myself at one point, but the horse-buying holiday was far more serious; I felt sick and was shitting myself the entire time and coughed up significantly more than the fiver I spent on antibiotics and Imodium in India.

Teeny tiny intestinal bugs might be an inconvenience, but they don't require stabling or saddles.

We didn't bring the pony back on that first trip to see it; it's a serious business buying a whole horse, and a lengthy one too, what with vet's assessments, x-rays etc etc. Also, a horse is a big ol' thing, and you can't just stick it in your bag with the passports and travel sweets. So we came home without it, and once CC2 was safely tucked up in bed, all excited from the trip abroad, CC1 and I had the Serious Chat. She told me that this new nag would be perfect for CC2 and that she loved it, but she understood it was a serious financial commitment to buy the thing and wanted to be sure I was 100% OK with the idea of spending all my money on it. I told her I absolutely wasn't, God no, but we compromised and I agreed to buy it anyway.

After all the formalities were taken care of a few days later, the moment finally arrived when I had to part with the cash. The money and I were left alone for a few moments of privacy as we said our goodbyes, and I don't mind admitting that I shed a tear or two. As a young man, I watched as friends of mine settled down one by one and hatched their nest eggs, but I never thought I'd have savings of my own. I watched as mine grew from a tiny little pile of notes no bigger than my fist, to a fully grown investment with its own personality, my heart swelling with pride as it did so. But the time comes in every man's life when he has to step aside and let the fruit of his loins spread its wings and move out, but I confess that it's left a large hole in my life. Empty nest egg syndrome, I believe it's called.

As it was a foreign nag (comin' over 'ere, takin' our sugarlumps and walkin' our circles), I had to pay in Euros, and naturally, I'd have preferred a nice, strong pound to make it cheaper. As it was, the pound had been looking pretty good for weeks, apart from one brief period where it dropped horribly, only to recover strongly about 20 minutes later. You can probably guess at what point I made the transaction, can't you? Yes, that's right, I chose the worst individual hour, possibly even minute, of the previous six months to make the transaction.

The conversation with the nag seller went much like this:

Me: How much is that horse?

Nag seller: Which one?

Me: The brown one, natch.

Nag seller: Oh, it's quite a lot.

Me: Right, course it is. Well, I'll buy it anyway, apparently.

Nag seller: OK, cool, here's the bill.

Me: Wow, that is a lot, isn't it? But needs must, so ok.

Nag seller: Bear in mind, you'll have to convert that into pounds to get the final figure.

Me: Ah yes, of course. And what's the current exchange rate?

Nag seller: *Checks phone* Absolutely dreadful. Worst for weeks. I'm afraid it's much more expensive than you even feared.

Me: Oh FFS. Well, here you are.

Nag seller: Thanks. *Checks phone again* Oh, it's all better again now. If only you'd waited another 14 seconds.

Me: FML

Once the payment was over and I'd recovered sufficiently, the new nag had to be picked up and driven home. You'd think I'd have been allowed to drive it home myself to ensure that the transition went as smoothly as possible, but it was explained to me that somebody would need to stay at home to look after the house and the various animals, and so it was decided that the two CCs would drive off to Europe to pick up the pony while I minded shop at home.

The "various animals" didn't just include pets though, but also the existing loan pony, and so I was forced into actually spending some quality time with a horse. I was given written instructions and even taken down to the hotel to be given practical lessons in basic nag care, which essentially involved sticking a rope thing on it and taking it outside into its field in the morning, plus a few pointers on how to move hay from Point A (the big pile of hay) to Point B (the horse). I turned up to class and made revision notes, but I wasn't really listening, if I'm being honest. I was mainly looking out the window and daydreaming, or writing rude words on a calculator.

I stayed up late the night before to do some cramming, and was loosely ready for the big day when it came, though CC2 was clearly terrified at the prospect of entrusting the pony's care to me. I think she feared that being left to my own devices for the night I'd be in a wine coma by about 3 pm and would forget to feed the nag in the evening, which was a very real risk, so I made a mental note to give it an extra large breakfast.

You'd probably assume that there would have been some shit-picking and stuff too, but I didn't have to do that in the end. No, I think CC1 feared my response if she asked me to get involved with the rear-end business and so decided to pay someone to come and do those bits for me. Of course, when I say "she paid someone" I mean that I paid someone, and although I was more than happy not to do any of the work, I was slightly miffed that I wasn't considered trustworthy to look after the nag in full. CC1 told me she was more than happy to give me the fifteen quid instead and not bother getting someone in, which I worked out would involve me paying myself my own money to clear up shit, so I concurred with her in the end and just let someone else do it.

And so off they went, trundling towards the horizon in

an expensive-yet-empty hired lorry to cross the channel on the ferry, returning the next day in an expensive-and-now-full-of-horse hired lorry. I, on the other hand, had to get up early to let the chickens out, let the cats in, let the dogs out, let the cats back in again, feed everything, herd the cats from room to room so they could eat and shit without, ideally, coming into contact with one another, and so on and so on. Plus, I had to make the many trips back and forth to the nag hotel to move the hay around.

I suspect the CCs were expecting *that* phone call: 'Er, it's me. I think I put the lead thing on wrong and then it sort of spooked and ran off into the woods. I don't think we'll see it again. But you're bringing that new one back, so we've still got one, right? Hello?'

But in the end, everything went as planned. The CCs arrived home, tired but happy with a new horse in the boot, and nothing died on my watch, so it was a success all round. And overnight, just like that, I became a horse owner.

CC1 keeps telling me that as I've bought a nag, I will now be invited into owners' enclosures at big prancing events and plied with free champagne. I don't know if this is real or not, but even if it is, CC2 is going to have to up her game in terms of the quality of competitions she enters. At all the ones I've been to I consider myself lucky if I can buy myself a can of warm Coke, and the only enclosures I've seen are the dusty areas next to the horse pitch where there's usually about three bored-looking parents staring into space.

You'd think that buying this new nag would mean that we could now give the old one back, wouldn't you? I mean, why does anyone need more than one horse at a time? Well, CC1's take on this is 'one wash, one wear,' and that if one breaks down, then there's always a spare one to use instead, so now we have two of the damned things. In an ideal world, this would be lovely — a choice of two little brown ponies to ride, one a boy horse and one a girl horse. If viral video clips on the internet have taught me anything, it's that when you put two animals together, they instantly fall in love and become inseparable pals, regardless of what species they are. It could be a dog and a cat, a goat and a monkey, or a polar bear and a jellyfish; as soon as two animals are thrust together then they start giving each other rides and grooming each other constantly, to the sound of uplifting music.

Putting two horses together ought to be a guaranteed love-in then, you'd assume, but in our case, the reality was that the old pony took an instant dislike to the new interloper. I think the official veterinary lingo here is 'hates its fucking guts.' I'm assuming word must've got out in the yard that a new horse was in town, and she got jealous. She was probably scared of being replaced by a new, younger model that could walk in even straighter lines, and so was a right little bitch to the new one, the poor thing, and kept trying to bite him. This wasn't really how I imagined horse ownership would be, but then to be fair, I've never actually imagined horse ownership at all. Whenever I head to the nag hotel now, I assume I'm going to have to be like the sensible drunk in a pub fight, standing between them both with outstretched arms, telling them how it ain't worth it and to settle down and have another drink.

CC2 had to do a bit of learning too, as it transpires that new, young ponies don't necessarily come out of the womb enjoying having young girls hanging off them, kissing them, nuzzling them and all that other weird shit she inflicts on them. The new nag even gave her a bit of a kick early on to keep her in line, though I imagine the whole experience of new ownership was quite traumatic for it — effectively kidnapped by a bunch of weird foreigners, bundled into the back of a lorry, driven for hundreds of miles and then stuck in a strange hotel room next door to someone that wants to kill him. I'd be the same.

Still, he made friends too and has a new best bud that he hangs out with, farting nonchalantly and discussing mares. He's supposed to live in the paddock next door, but they keep breaking into each other's to be closer, which is quite sweet. They then sort of cuddle and rub each other's necks, so I'm not sure in retrospect whether they're best mates or whether it's more like *Brokeback Mountain* without the humans, but as long as he's happy.

The other horse actually ran through the fence to be with our new nag at one point, which sounds dramatic at first, but fences in the horse world aren't always real ones made out of wood or metal, but just a bit of flimsy tape, so running through one is more like being the winner in a 100m sprint rather than doing anything that requires stunt work.

The new nag tried a different tack to be with his mate and surprised everyone by easily vaulting the fence by a clear foot or so, thus making us wonder whether dressage is actually the right discipline for him. Maybe he got wind of what he's supposed to be learning in the yard gossip and was like, 'Walking around in circles?! WTF?! Check this out, mofos!'

CC2 fell deeply in love with him immediately, but then he's a horse and so that's a given. She didn't even mind being kicked by it but took it as a sign of affection because she's an idiot like that and considers all horses to be perfect. If she owned a slavering hellhorse with multiple rows of blood-stained, gnashing teeth that had already ripped two of her limbs off, she'd describe it as 'an adorable little dumpling of a luvvly, wuvvly ponykins that's maybe a teeny bit bitey,' and then promptly try to feed it a carrot from her mouth. She'll never learn.

She does, however, refer to him constantly as 'your pony', which is a surprise to me given how proprietorial she is generally with the nags. Of course, it makes more sense in context...

'Oh by the way, *your pony* needs new travel boots,' was the first thing she said to me when they got home with him, and there have been several similar utterances since. She'll come home from shit-picking or similar, and saunter past me sitting at the kitchen table reading the bills with a casual '*your pony* needs a new saddle by the way,' or, 'it's cold outside and *your pony* doesn't have a warm rug — do you want him to be cold?'

This is all emotional blackmail, of course, and I assume she thinks that I'm going to be a bit easier with the purse strings now that I've ploughed money into my own personal investment. Well, that's lovely and everything, but there's no money left. I burnt the purse strings along with the purse to keep us warm and the piggy bank is now 90% Sellotape and failing to stand upright.

But still, I don't need to pay bills any more, or eat. Because I have my own horse. And as you know, that's all I've ever wanted!

CC2 was naturally very excited at the purchase and wasted no time in making plans. She told me with a straight face that the sensible thing would be to have them both come to live with us at home in order to save hotel costs. She confused me at first by suggesting that if I sold off the rusting pile of green metal I keep, then we'd have more disposable money. I had to scratch my head at that one.

'Rusting pile of green metal? What rusting pile of green metal?' I asked her.

'You know, in the garage,' she replied. I had to think for a second, visualising the various bits of crap stored in there.

'I'm sorry, are you talking about my car??'

'Yes. If you sold that, then not only would we have more money, but a perfect stable. That garage could be turned into two lovely loose boxes. We just need to fit some proper doors on it.'

FFS.

My view on nag ownership has always been that it's something I'd never have to face. It was something other people did — people with a lot more money than me, and/or bits of horse shit under their nails. I was very much of the opinion that it would be a cold day in hell before I ever bought a horse.

Well, I'm now in hell. Could someone pop the heater on?

If it flies, floats or foals
Always rent it
It's bound to cost you less cash in the end

The person who first said this
Must've meant it
Even though he had much more than me to spend

The problem is the high cost
If you dent it
You have to think how much it costs to mend

There'll be no money left
Because you spent it
And this advice is free to you, my friend

CHAPTER 9

Don't give up all hope

DON'T GIVE UP ALL HOPE

I imagine by this point, you're probably thinking that horse people are a completely lost cause and that if you let one into your life, then any hope you have of staying sane, staying safe or staying out of your overdraft is gone. And, well, yeah, that's pretty much the size of it.

But it's important to be positive in life and to look at the nag world in a 'bucket half full' kind of way. You've probably already come to the conclusion that I'm a pretty positive sort of guy myself, who's embraced the whole nag thing will a great deal of enthusiasm and optimism. To that end, I'm going to give you a little quiz to do now — it might not seem very relevant to start with, but I have a point to make in a very roundabout sort of way, so stick with me!

HAVE YOU GOT A TEENAGER LIVING IN YOUR HOUSE?

You can often tell, but if you're unsure, then answer the following:

QUESTION I

When you've put all the crockery and cutlery away from the dishwasher, how many of each item do you now have in the cupboards?

A. Why, all of them, of course. The full 24-place setting that we got on our wedding day, plus a few extras picked up here and there over the years.

B. Plenty. It's mainly non-matching bits of Ikea crap we bought as a 'temporary' solution 20 years ago, but there's enough for everyone.

C. Fuck all. I know we own at least a dozen of everything, but I don't know where they go. We only seem to be left with a few knives and that comedy mug that someone gave us for Christmas one year which, despite being slightly rude, is just too small for a satisfying cuppa. God knows where it all goes. I dream about teaspoons.

QUESTION 2

If you leave a phone charging cable attached to a wall plug in a public space (kitchen, living room etc), how long will it stay there?

A. Forever! I've only ever used the one that came in the box and it's provided sterling service over the years.

B. A few months, but I keep having to replace them, it seems. Sometimes they break, sometimes someone seems to 'borrow' one, and it gets lost.

C. About 3 and a half minutes. I bought a 10-pack of Amazon Basics ones only this morning and they'd all gone by lunchtime. I think someone's selling them for drugs.

QUESTION 3

It's wash day! You let everyone in the house know that you're going to do all the washing, but they need to bring everything downstairs. If you were to go to each bedroom in turn, how much dirty washing would you still find?

A. None. To be honest, everyone tends to just bring theirs down every day anyway and puts it in the basket in the laundry room, so it's all ready and waiting. Or else they wash it themselves.

B. A few bits and pieces. Probably the odd towel and loose sock strewn on the floor somewhere, but generally everyone's pretty good.

C. All of it. More than all of it, in fact, because I'll find clothes that don't even belong to them. So, on average, around 110% of all the clothes they own. They'll all be on the floor too, despite me buying perfectly good laundry baskets for each bedroom. Those will be full too, though. Of dirty bowls.

QUESTION 4

What time does everyone get up by each day?

A. About 6:30 am at the latest. Early morning is the best time of day, and we're usually all out by then on our brisk, pre-breakfast walk.

B. Pre-lockdown about 7:30 am. Post-lockdown about 8:56.

C. It depends on where you define the start of the day. If someone gets up at 6 pm but stays up until the early hours, is that late on one day or just very early on the next?

QUESTION 5

On weekends and school holidays, is everyone busy and out of the house during the day?

A. Yes, we all work. And if not, then there's plenty of gardening and DIY to be getting on with around the house and gardens. Nobody's idle.

B. Pretty much. Everyone seems to find something to do, even if it's just going and hanging out by the shops.

C. No. There are bodies everywhere, occupying any horizontal surface. If you need someone, you just go to the nearest plug point and follow the extension cable like a modern-day Hansel and Gretel until you find a phone at the end of it in some grubby paw.

HOW DID YOU DO?

If you scored mainly A's then you can be pretty certain that you don't have any teenagers living in your house, which is nice. On the flip side, though, I don't know who you are... you're definitely no friend of mine.

If you scored mainly B's then you probably don't have any teenagers, but it sounds like you do have some children. They could be in their twenties, in which case you need to be hurrying them along a bit. They don't sound like much bother but, y'know, enough's enough. Alternatively, you might have younger children still. Which is nice. For now.

If you scored mainly C's, then I'm afraid there's a very strong possibility that you have some teenagers living with you. They may be yours, they may be someone else's. It's sometimes hard to tell what's lurking under a hoodie or behind that fringe. But that £150 Tesco shop is gonna last about an hour, that's all I'm saying.

And this leads us onto our own, dear, CC2. She's the Archetypal Teen in many ways. She complains constantly that she needs a new phone with better battery life, seemingly unaware that 8 hours of Netflix isn't considered normal usage... before midday. She's got the storming off/slamming door routine down just so and she's even almost convinced us that oh my God, her life's sooo unfaaair. And god knows what she does with all the spoons and phone cables, it's a complete mystery.

But here's the thing. She wouldn't score all C's on that test, not by a long shot. Because horses. Let me explain.

We all know that teenagers are almost impossible to wake up in the morning. Or afternoon. They go into some kind of hibernation mode for half the day where they manage to shut down their bodies into some weird unconscious state that's closer to death than to life, and the usual techniques of employing alarm clocks or trying to shake them awake have no effect. So, what time does CC2 get up, in the school holidays at least? What time does she drag her teenaged self out of her (admittedly rank) pit every morning?

About 5 am. Seriously.

She'll be badgering CC1 for a lift to the nag hotel by 5:30 so she can ride the pony before it gets too warm. Yup, that's right. She's there at dawn every morning, tacking out and mucking in and bringing this and that out or in and stuff about buckets. I'm hazy on the details. She's even been having lessons via Zoom, at 7 am. The poor bloody trainer — though in fairness, she probably did it from bed.

This is all good and well, you might be thinking, but it's still a cripplingly expensive hobby, isn't it? Having a child get up early is all good and well, but it doesn't pay the bills. And, well, yes, there's no getting away from it — let a horse person into your life and you can forget about nice, foreign holidays for a while unless they're the kind where you go abroad to look at a horse they want to buy. The expenses are both expensive and expansive.

CC2 got a new nag hat recently, for example. She's been banging on about it for months, and I really mean months. Every dinner time she's been getting her phone out, showing us photos and asking our opinion, just so she can then ignore it. Blue or black? This brand or that brand? Fake crystals glued all over or just glued all over the top bit? Etc, etc, etc.

Frankly, I just zone out and let CC1 handle things. Discussing the inner lining material of potential nag hats is most definitely a pink job, so I just sit back, pour another glass of wine and wonder how much this is all going to cost me.

Finally, we reached crunch time — the decisions were

all made, the spec was settled on and the financial trigger was pulled. And CC2 got a shiny new hat.

So, I hear you ask, what's she got? What colour is it? Where are the fake crystals positioned? What's the lining like? Fuck knows. Couldn't give a shit. All I know is that it cost a fortune. A ridiculous amount of money, seriously. Now, I like motorbikes and so I'm quite familiar with the exorbitant cost of helmets. But bike helmets are designed to go scraping down tarmac at 100mph, not grazing sawdust at 4mph, so I assume those crystals are diamonds.

You'd probably expect me to be really pissed off that I had to fork out for this overpriced piece of plastic with its hugely expensive logo stuck on the front?

Well, no actually. Because I didn't buy it. CC2 did. With her own money. You see, she hasn't just been getting up early in the holidays to ride the pony and stroke it all day, she's also been working down there. She goes freelance and does all the jobs for endless other ponies too, who have sensible owners that like lie-ins. She gets dropped down there at 5:30 am, sometimes comes back for lunch if there's no packed lunch for her, and then we pick her up again late evening. And in she strolls, happy as Larry, reeking of horse piss and smiling broadly, at least until she remembers that there are no horses in the house.

She can rake it in, too, and not just the shit either, I mean actual money. She declared herself a 'breadwinner' the other day, but I had to point out that technically that comes from contributing to the household, not just saving for her own stuff. I'm fighting hard not to tap her for fifty quid until I get paid, to be honest. It's not right.

Now, I'd have never spent as much money as she did on the hat, but who am I to complain? It's her money and she can do with it what she pleases. And frankly, I'd much rather she spent it on fake crystals than, say, drugs and vodka. Or even iPhone games. Or pretty much anything, really. Her all-encompassing passion in life is nags and if she wants to spend everything she has on a shiny new hat, then good luck to her!

I'm actually very proud; she saved up for years and bought something she loves that helps her with her chosen sport. Good for her. It's shown dedication, patience, discipline and self-control. Though mainly I'm just pleased I didn't have to buy it myself.

I'm not naive enough to think that this means she's now contributing in any meaningful way to the nag expenses. Her money is all spent now, and I imagine it'll be a fair while before she manages to amass that kind of quantity again. It'll be many years before we stop paying all the expenses, assuming we ever do completely. I'll probably be in a nursing home in my 90s, trying to hold out until the next advert break in Cash in the Attic for a wee, and working out how much I can sell my Zimmer frame for to buy matchy matchy shit for her.

But still... she has a passion in life that she adores, and isn't life pretty much just about this? Big houses and nice cars are all very well, but if you have something that drives you to leap out of bed every morning with energy and excitement, desperate to get on with the very thing that you live for, isn't that all anyone really wants? Not only that, but this in turn has led to her being diligent, hard-working, dedicated, committed and out of the house by 5:30. My kind of child!

If this continues, and I see no reason why it won't, then she'll grow up to be an incredible young woman with drive and focus and passion, who works hard to get what she wants, participates in her sport at the highest, most competitive level and continues to live with a fire burning in her heart for her love of horses. And frankly, when all's said and done, and all my whingeing is over, that's alright by me. I couldn't be prouder and I look forward to many years ahead of being prouder still.

In the meantime, I just need to find out where she's hiding all the spoons. Probably in the same drawer she stashes all the iPhone cables she's selling for crack.

GLOSSARY

Nagknot

GLOSSARY

Brown
The colour of almost all horses. Admittedly, a few are whiteish and some are black, but the rest are just shades of brown, despite what anyone tells you.

Bucket
The most useful equine accessory in the world. It's important to own at least 100 of these in case you need to store any mouldy old brushes, fetid water or actual shit for the rest of time.

Canter banter
The endless and inane chit-chat over the dinner table about what colour numbnuts to buy next. *SEE Numbnut, SEE Rug chat*

Car
What the horse was replaced with in 1886, but is now used to tow horses around with.

CC1
Cost Centre One. My other half, mother of our child and general financial burden to me.

CC2
Cost Centre Two. Our horse-mad, 14-year-old daughter, whose addiction to nags, dressage and matchy matchy is the ruin of me.

Charlotte of the Garden
Charlotte of the Garden is a world-famous prancer and CC2's hero. She saw her once at Olympia and practically assaulted her in trying to get a selfie taken.

Chin groove
Part of a horse's head. *SEE John Travolta*

Cool mule
A very good horse.

Dark horse
A secret 'extra' horse owned out of sight of the owner's significant other. Not to be confused with a brown horse.

Fartle
A fart followed by a startled horse. The fart could be from you, the horse, or any one else nearby, either human or naguine. *SEE Naguine*

Formal prancing
Doing prancing in front of an actual old lady judge at a competition. *SEE Prancing*

Fwerp
The noise a boy horse makes as air is expelled from his bits as he walks.

Horsesome
When something nag-related is particularly good.

Horse stroking
The main activity of horse owners, after buying things. Countless hours can be whiled away, stroking the horse with a collection of different brushes and other implements. Or, if none are to hand, then just stroking with bear hands while nuzzling into its neck.

Horse tax
The additional 100% tax that's added on top of the standard purchase price of any item, object or service that is sold in connection with a horse. For example, a standard apple might be sold for 60p, but if it's intended for a horse then it will be sold for £1.20. The tax is collected by the government's Department of Equine Affairs.

Impulsion
The urge to buy matchy matchy shit. *SEE Matchy matchy*

Lame
A horse with a hurty leg. Also dressage.

Leg warmers
80s-style fashion accessory, popular with trendy disco horses.

Matchy matchy

Dressing your horse up like it's a doll.

Nagaddict

A person whose life revolves around the owning, cleaning, brushing, breeding, stroking of, cleaning up after, and sometimes riding, horses.

Naganomics

Naguine financial accounting. *SEE Naguine*

Nagaphernalia

All the shit that comes with a horse and ends up filling the entirety of your car boot and several rooms of your house.

Nagated

Made ineffective or useless by the all-consuming power of a nearby horse.

Nagative

Something bad about horses. *SEE pages 1-155 for details.*

Nag Fund

The financial fund that contains a special one-way valve, enabling money to enter but never leave. *SEE Naganomics, SEE Hotel California*

Nag hat

A crown that horse people wear, but slightly more expensive.

Nag hotel

The luxury accommodation that horses hang out in.

Nagknot
A pile of leg warmers that are fresh out of the tumble dryer. The Rubik's Cube of the nag world; the world record for untangling one is 2 hours and 17 minutes, held by a 12-year-old Hungarian rider.

Naglet
A young horse.

Nagmag
Glossy magazines for Nag addicts.

Nagmas
That special time of year when horses finally have a day off to chill out, chat amongst themselves and gorge on carrots.

Nagmagnets
Standard fridge magnets that have been imbued with magical healing powers by a horse shaman.

Naguine
Adjective to describe horse-related stuff.

Neigh
The noise a horse makes. Also what you should say if someone in your family asks you to buy a horse for them.

Neighsayer
One who speaks fluent horse.

Nightmare
A female horse that only comes out after dark.

Numbnut

The thing that goes under the saddle. Used to match colours with the other horse clothes and for showing off the 'sponsorship' you got from your dad's company.

Overdraft

Collective noun for a group of horses. E.g. Oh look, there's a beautiful overdraft of wild ponies running across that moor.

Pitch

Any area within which horse games are played.

Prancing

Walking your horse from one letter to another, or perhaps in circles when you get better at it. *SEE Formal prancing*

Quarter horse

A very small horse, such as a Shetland.

Rigging

All the bits of leather and rope that are strapped onto and around the horse to hold everything in place and give you something to hold onto.

Rug chat

A specific portion of the *Canter banter* that's dedicated to the discussion of rug strategy. *SEE Canter banter, RugTech*

RugTech

The branch of material technology that enables one person to own 43 different horse rugs for each change in a single degree of ambient temperature. *SEE Rug chat*

Salt
One of the key ingredients that horses seem to require in vast quantities for reasons medical science hasn't yet found the answer to.

Seahorse
A horse that's a strong swimmer.

Sportscow
A horse.

THE END

You got to the end, congratulations!

If you enjoyed this book, please, please do consider leaving a review on Amazon — it makes a huge difference to small, self-published authors like me who rely entirely on word-of-mouth.

When I say 'small', I don't mean in stature necessarily, I just mean in terms of staff (zero) and marketing budget (zero). I'm an entirely normal height, honestly.

If you're a member of Goodreads, then that's also a lovely place to leave a review. Any mentions on social media are obviously immensely appreciated too.

That's it, begging over.

If you didn't enjoy this book then I'm very, very sorry. I'm not sure what we do now, it's all got a bit awkward. You could burn it I suppose, if that'll make you feel any better? I won't mind. Don't do this if you're reading the Kindle version though, that would be a terrible mistake. Alternatively, if you really thought it was awful and that nobody could possibly enjoy it, you could just give it to someone you don't like. They'll only stick it in the downstairs loo anyway, and that would be kind of fitting in this case.

If you'd like to read more of this kind of nonsense on a regular basis, then do follow me on my Facebook page where I post regularly about the day-to-day goings on with CC1, CC2 and the nags.

I also post some stuff on Instagram and Twitter occasionally, though I often forget to. Please follow me wherever you like.

On top of that, you can sign up to my newsletter and receive incredibly sporadic updates about any new books or other big news. I won't spam you, I promise. In fact, I send about one email every couple of years, I should really do more with it. But there you go. You can sign up from my website or from my Facebook page, in theory at least. It might be broken, I'll check.

 @skintdressagedaddy

 @skintdressagedaddy

 @dressagedaddy

 www.skintdressagedaddy.com

"Follow one man's journey into misery, mild alcohol dependence and, ultimately, probable financial ruin as he hilariously explains everything you need to know about the world of horses and horse sports."

The first Skint Dressage Daddy book, ***From Nags to Numbnuts***, (an Amazon bestseller in both the UK and Australia) is available in paperback and Kindle.

Search on Amazon or go to www.skintdressagedaddy.com.

REVIEWS

"Fabulous, wonderful, exceedingly well written"

"It's priceless, I've not stopped crying with laughter"

"I just couldn't put it down!!!""So many moments of hysterical giggles and tears"

"Received mine, my other half pinched it and loves it"

*"It's f****** hilarious"*

"LOVING IT!"

"Eager to read more but also not wanting it to end!"

"Bloody brilliant!"

If you enjoyed this book but thought it needed a bit more animation, then **Nag Hotel** may be just your thing.

Follow the adventures of Prince and Geoffrey, the miserable old codger and his hapless 'friend', as they stagger from one disaster to another.

There are two seasons of episodes and they're only a couple of minutes long each, so you don't waste too much time... though there's also a Christmas Special that's a feature-length 9 minutes!

Contains swearing and references to smoking, drinking, drugs, sex & violence. Suitable for all ages.

youtube.com/skintdressagedaddy

(Season 3 *may* be coming in 2022!)

If you'd like to share your own amusing nag-related photos, videos, jokes or anecdotes, then join the **Nagland** group on Facebook.

It's basically just a load of horse people sharing fun and funny horse stuff from themselves and around the internet.

Go to **facebook.com/groups/naglandgroup**